ESTHER
QUEEN OF PERSIA

PATRICIA HERDOIZA HERNÁNDEZ

ISBN 979-8-88644-854-2 (Paperback)
ISBN 979-8-88644-855-9 (Digital)

Covenant Books
11661 Hwy 707
Murrells Inlet, SC 29576
www.covenantbooks.com

The following is an imagined retelling of the story of Esther from the Bible.

To survivors of generational and multigenerational trauma

To anyone who feels they have to hide who they
are, especially from someone they love

DISCLAIMER

The author of this story is not particularly concerned with historical details. As explained in the "Purpose of Writing" section, she is telling this story as it speaks to her via a psychological as well as spiritual lens. While the Bible story of Esther is used as the main framework from which this story flows, the author has changed certain details such as time frames. Specifically, the four-year period between Vashti's demotion and Esther and Xerxes's marriage has been taken out. Additionally, the five-year period between Esther marrying Xerxes and the events surrounding Haman's plot has been shortened to one year for simplification and storytelling purposes. Lastly, for purposes of this retelling, the author has maintained the simplicity and familiarity of Esther's better-known name, *Esther*, as opposed to her initially mentioned Hebrew name, *Hadassah*, in the book of Esther (Esther 2:7). She has done this since Esther is called *Esther* throughout the entirety of the book bearing this same name in the Bible, so it is the name people are more familiar with. In order to maintain connection to Esther's Hebrew roots, however, the author has also defined the meaning of the name *Esther* in this retelling as the same as her Hebrew name *Hadassah*: "myrtle tree."

Advisory

Given the account of Esther, this retelling will contain a degree of mature content. The author portrays a story of healthy romantic as well as sacrificial love forming between Esther and Xerxes. While nothing is mentioned that the author deems explicit or inappropriate, this content may still be too sensitive for some readers. Reader discretion is advised, particularly with regard to chapters 8 and 9, in which Esther and then Xerxes reflect on their wedding night.

CONTENTS

PURPOSE OF WRITING

To connect with the story from Scripture on a human level while learning spiritual lessons throughout. Esther, Mordecai, Xerxes, Hegai, Hathak, Vashti, and others are people who lived long ago and in a very different context from ours today. Yet at their core, they were human beings just like us, with thoughts, emotions, beliefs, relationships, and a sense of humor in life. Let's delve deep into their lives to learn spiritual as well as psychological lessons about being human, regardless of context.

God clearly has a sense of humor, as indicated by His many uses of sarcasm and other literary devices in the Bible. We, as human beings, also have a sense of humor, which isn't surprising, given that God made us in His image (Gen. 1:27). Since we know there is nothing truly new under the sun (Eccles. 1:9), there is no reason we can't relate to the people in this story and other Bible accounts. In doing so, we enrich our lives not only by connecting with the incredible events they lived firsthand, but ultimately by learning more about God, our Creator and Father. The book of Esther in the Bible does not mention God, but of course, God was with her at every moment, and she knew it. God is also always with you.

The story of Esther and Xerxes presents a unique opportunity for spiritual as well as personal growth if we truly absorb it. As a Christian, I personally believe King Xerxes represents God in the story, and Queen Esther represents God's people. Furthermore, I believe that despite the very different customs of their day compared to ours (harems with multiple wives for a king, some men made into eunuchs, women are married to the king at first sight, etc.), the spiritual principles in the story are timeless. All that being said, of course we understand that this couple is a man and a woman, human beings just like us who are not perfect and, in fact, have many flaws.

From the human perspective, therefore, we can learn so much from these two people. As a human being who also happens to be a professor of psychology, I am very interested in helping people (including myself!) by teaching about healthy relationships. Esther and Xerxes struggle but ultimately do show up for each other, and in so doing, they become our example. One lesson to be learned from them is that all of us have baggage, scars, or trauma. Celebrate the beauty of being vulnerable with your beloved. Really listen to each other. Don't judge or push your marriage partner away. Instead, give them grace.

The Bible story of Esther is used as the main inspiration and outline for this writing. Another source of inspiration is the novel *The Hate U Give* by Angie Thomas, concerning racial, personal, and generational trauma and safety rules passed down in families. The account of Esther recorded in Scripture is widely regarded as fascinating and even perplexing due to being so distinct from other books of the Bible. As we tell this story in an imagined way, which makes sense to the author, let's consider all we can learn from this treasured tale. The text of the book of Esther is included at the end for reference, and a section of Bible references is also included by chapter. May you be blessed as you read this book. Enjoy!

Additional Literary and Other Allusions

The first chapter of this book is titled "A Myrtle Tree Grows in Persia," which is a reference to the novel *A Tree Grows in Brooklyn* by Betty Smith. This classic book about Francie Nolan and her family portrays themes of hope despite hardship, which is also what Esther experiences in this retelling. The sixth chapter, "Father of the Bride," receives its title from the film by the same name starring Steve Martin and Diane Keaton. This movie is a lighthearted and humorous portrayal about a man reluctantly giving his daughter away in marriage in modern times, while in the author's retelling of Esther, Mordecai is also forced to do so but under very different circumstances. Chapter

7 of *Esther: Queen of Persia* is titled "One Night with the King," which is a reference to the film *One Night with the King* (same title) directed by Michael O. Sajbel. This film is also about Esther's story. Chapter 8 of this retelling of Esther is called "Decision Day," which is inspired by the reality TV show *Married at First Sight* on Lifetime channel. In this show, people are matched by professional match-makers, including a sociologist, therapist, and pastor. The couple is then married at first sight and after being married for a period of eight weeks, it is "decision day" in which they decide to stay married or get divorced.

In *Esther: Queen of Persia*, Esther and Xerxes are married at first sight as well, having been matched by God orchestrating their lives behind the scenes so to speak. Xerxes' decision the morning after their wedding night is not whether they will stay together, but rather if Esther will be simply a new wife or his queen bride. Perhaps this is because, in Bible times, people had more commitment and respect in marriage, not as something to "try out" but as something to work at respectfully with their marriage partner. While it may be strange for us in modern times to consider being married at first sight (despite the existence of the reality TV show!), this was the situation Esther and Xerxes experienced in their day.

The author presents their wedding night as planting the seeds for the necessary ingredients in marriage, recognized today in the field of psychology. According to the triangular theory of love proposed by psychologist Robert J. Sternberg, these three necessary ingredients are passion, commitment, and intimacy. As we see in the story, Esther and Xerxes feel passion toward each other when they have a mutual physical attraction upon seeing each other. They are also committed upon seeing each other, as this is their wedding night; and they are, therefore, married, marriage being something binding and permanent in their day and culture. In their conversation at the table, they speak openly with one another, achieving a decent amount of intimacy thereby. Hence, even though the timeline is very quick, one night together, it is possible for them to see they will have a good marriage, and therefore Xerxes makes the wise decision to make Esther his queen wife. Lastly, chapter 17, "God Save the

King," is a reference to the British national anthem, "God Save the Queen." In this retelling, it is the queen who risks her life to save the king in that part of Esther's story.

ACKNOWLEDGMENTS

I would like to thank my mom, Mary Catherine, who has always been encouraging in my faith journey and has enjoyed reading my spiritual writings. Love you, Mommy!

A million thanks to my best friend Garvi who read my first drafts, shared my enthusiasm, gave helpful feedback, and offered invaluable perspective! Girl, you're the best, and you always have been! Thank you so much!

Many thanks to my beloved husband, Elías! Babe, I am so in love with you! I'm so glad and thankful God brought us together as man and wife. Thanks for being supportive of this and my other spiritual projects because, in your words, I like doing this, and I can do this, so therefore, I might as well do it. Gracias, bebé! Te amo tanto! You're the Xerxes to my Esther.

Thanks a million times over to my dear, deceased brother in faith! A fellow former Catholic who also chose to become Christadelphian as an adult, he understood this journey and was so inspiring to many. When I wrote my letter requesting baptism, he said I had written "a wee book." Now I have written an actual book. The reason I have done this is to share with the world how we believe in a "divine benevolent monarchy to come," as you once described. We wait for the return of Jesus to be King of the earth, in a sense foreshadowed in the love story of Esther and King Xerxes. I am so looking forward to seeing him again after the resurrection! We will sing a favorite hymn about how God's mercies are "new every morning" and "great is Thy faithfulness!" Indeed, what a blessed resurrection morning that will be! Amen!

Thanks to my students, who occasionally enjoyed hearing me "geek out" about my writing process, from a psychological perspective.

Thank you to Christ my King, son of God! He is my friend, example, mediator, leader, teacher, savior, and brother. May this book point more people toward You, I pray. Jesus, You said we are the light of the world and to not keep our light hidden under a bowl (Matt. 5:14–16), and so I'm not; I'm sharing it with the world!

> You are the light of the world. A town built on a hill cannot be hidden. Neither do people light a lamp and put it under a bowl. Instead, they put it on its stand, and it gives light to everyone in the house. In the same way, let your light shine before others, that they may see your good deeds and glorify your Father in heaven. (Matt. 5:14–16)

INTRODUCTION

As you read this story, consider the following Bible quotes:

> You came to the Kingdom for such a time as this. (Esther 4:14)

> A time to be silent and a time to speak. (Eccles. 3:7)

PROLOGUE

After the kingdom of Israel split in two and was taken into Assyrian and then Babylonian captivity, the Persian Empire grew into a world power. Esther and her uncle Mordecai are Jews who live in Persia. Mordecai has raised Esther since being orphaned himself followed by Esther's parents also being killed for being Jews in a foreign land.

CHAPTER I

A Myrtle Tree Grows in Persia

"No! Nooo! Nooo!" Esther heard the screams before she opened her eyes. Getting up quickly, she grabbed a cloth, dipped it in water, and ran to her uncle's room. Mordecai was flailing and sweating on his bed. As she held him down and rubbed the cloth on his forehead, he gradually calmed and woke up.

"Esther! Esther!"

"It's okay, Uncle. I'm here, I'm here, everything is fine!"

He stopped flailing and calmed his breathing. The birds outside were chirping. Mordecai focused on that, a trick he'd used many times to help refocus and relax.

"The same nightmare, right?" Esther wondered why she even asked. It had been the same since she was a little girl, too young to remember the murder of her parents, along with Mordecai's.

Mordecai looked at his niece, the only person left in their family. He had been young when their parents were killed, and she was only three at the time. Sixteen years later and nightmares were still a recurring event in their home. Mordecai could only thank God Esther had been too young to recall what he'd witnessed on that horrendous day.

That day constantly played back in his mind. His parents and hers always kept them inside the house for fear of persecution, just in case anyone found out they were Jews. Mordecai was thirteen the day armed soldiers showed up at the door, apparently out to get the

Jews, and slaughtered Mordecai's parents, along with Esther's, right there on the doorstep! It was an absolute bloodbath!

Mordecai had snatched Esther up and taken off running, leaving out the back of the house. He didn't stop running until he was out of breath. He'd been crying, but what could he do! All he could do was save himself and Esther at that point! Life was always just a quest to survive. That night, he had returned with Esther; left her at his friend Leenah's home while he buried his parents, sister, and brother-in-law; and cried himself to sleep. God had protected them all this time since, and no one knew they were related to the people who had mysteriously disappeared all those years ago. That's because Mordecai and Esther had been hidden by their parents to keep them safe. Now Esther's safety was Mordecai's goal for life, as he'd raised her as his own daughter.

He sat up, wiped his tears, and lifted his hands.

"A new day, praise Yahweh!" Esther raised her hands up to the sky and nodded her head.

"I'll make us some breakfast, Uncle. You'll feel better." She went to the kitchen and squeezed some fruit to make juice, grabbing a few pieces of leftover bread from the night before. On days when Mordecai had nightmares, she just took anything she could from the night before to his room so they could eat together there. Best to let him calm down more. They ate in silence. Then it was time for Esther to go to work at the nearby bakery and Mordecai as a butcher. At the door, Mordecai stopped her, as usual.

"Recite the rules."

Esther took a deep breath. "Don't tell anyone I'm Jewish. Don't pray in public. Be obedient at all times, especially with authority."

"Right. These are the rules that keep us safe. God, we pray for our safety and security today and always, and for the coming of the Messiah to save us for all time. Amen."

"Amen!" It was always good when Mordecai moved on to praying after reciting those depressing rules. Esther knew why he had those rules, but it just wasn't what she wanted to think about. Esther liked to speak her mind and wanted to just live her life, but she knew not to talk about being Jewish. Other than that, she wished to be a free spirit. After all, Mom and Dad (God rest their souls) had named her after a myrtle tree, and she wasn't meant to just stay in the ground. She wanted to stretch her arms and bloom, just like a myrtle tree does.

Still, even as they went their separate ways to work, Esther couldn't help but glance down at the front steps of their home. For sixteen years, the blood of their parents stayed there; it had never come out. Sometimes, Esther wondered if Mordecai kept it there on purpose as a reminder, or if he couldn't bring himself to fully clean it up. Either way, it was there. A reminder of the constant threat hanging over their heads: Jews in a foreign land. Thankfully, Mordecai's profession as a butcher provided a convenient explanation if anyone ever asked about the blood. He'd just shrug and casually reply, "Hazards of the job." On the one hand, it hurt to have the memory of her parents and grandparents dismissed from Mordecai's mouth. On the other, God knew his heart and that her uncle was doing his best to protect them. Still, despite her best efforts and faith, sometimes Esther felt like a fish out of water instead of a tree planted in the ground and reaching up to God.

CHAPTER 2

All in a Day's Work

It was still early, so the sun wasn't completely up yet. *No matter,* Esther thought to herself, *God, Your word is a lamp to my feet and a light to my path.* Since Mordecai told her to not pray in public, it was always a habit to pray only in her mind. God knew her heart. She followed the path and went into the bakery.

The day went quickly; she helped bake and sell pies. Her boss, Leenah, always let her take the leftovers home. Leenah was such a kind soul. She was basically Esther's mom. She and Mordecai had been childhood friends, and it was Leenah who cared for baby Esther the night of the family murders. Of course, Esther didn't remember, but she kept this in her heart and never forgot all Leenah had done for her and her uncle.

It had been a rough morning for Mordecai. Esther wondered how he was doing. She hummed while she worked to distract herself.

"Esther, I wish I had your energy! I'm tired already!" Esther laughed at her boss's compliment. "You're so pretty, soon you'll be whipping up some nice food for a husband!" Esther dropped the rolling pin. Marriage? All she could think about was taking life one day at a time and trying to take care of her uncle.

"Sorry, I didn't mean to disturb your concentration, dear!"

Esther smiled weakly. "That's all right, Leenah. I just always thought of staying at home with my uncle. I don't know if marriage is for me."

"Ha! We'll see." Esther refocused on her work, and the hours went by. When she daydreamed, she always liked to imagine her future being very different. Maybe she and Mordecai would be able to move someday, somewhere safer for Jews. Maybe they could go to Israel, their promised land. Maybe the Messiah would come and save them once and for all, like her uncle had prayed that morning. Or maybe, just maybe, she would find, well, love. *Focus on work, Esther*, she told herself. Jews can't afford to dream, not here anyway.

Meanwhile, Mordecai arrived at his job. He was still sweating. He hated how he worried Esther with his nightmares. He purposely hadn't answered her question this morning. It wasn't the same nightmare, but a different one. He'd been having this one for a while now, a few months. In this dream, Esther was getting married, and her husband took out a sword instead of a ring. Mordecai had never been superstitious, and in the past, his nightmares had been about the past only. But this was new. *God, are You trying to tell me something? Is something bad about to happen?*

He tried to tell himself it was just nerves about Esther having grown up. In reality, she'd been a woman for a few years now, but it just seemed to have happened so fast! It felt like just yesterday she was a little girl running around the house, breaking his heart when she asked about where Mommy and Daddy were. She didn't remember her parents but still asked about them for a few years. He had waited till she was older to tell her the truth about what happened to them. Now she was a woman, and so beautiful. She looked just like her mom, his lovely big sister, God rest her soul. Sooner or later, some man would see her and want her for himself. Well, the rules would stay the same. No telling her husband she was Jewish. It wasn't fair. Why should Esther feel she had to take care of him and even if she were to find a man, not be able to be honest about who she was. *Either way, it's time to look toward her future and find her a husband,* Mordecai told himself.

God, please help me with this, he prayed.

CHAPTER 3

Big News

"I'm home!" Esther called as she shut the door. Mordecai was setting the table for dinner. She joined him.

"How was your day?" Mordecai furrowed his brow as he studied her face.

"Same as always, how was yours?" Was he worried about something? Why was he asking questions? Usually, they were both too exhausted to converse at all after work.

"Esther, I think we should talk about your future." Ah, of course, that's it. Esther hated how her uncle worried so much. The future would take care of itself somehow. Esther knew God would protect and provide no matter what, but she also tried not to think or dream too much about the future. It hurt too much since she didn't know what to expect or hope for.

"My future is here with you, same as it's always been, Uncle," she answered plainly.

The tone of her voice pained him. Why was she so resigned to taking care of him? Surely, a girl as lovely as Esther deserved more out of life. Had he really taken care of her all these years so she could simply turn around and do the same for him? It was a noble thing, her caring attitude, and he loved her for it. But part of his duty as her uncle was to make sure she'd be okay after his death. That meant securing her a husband.

"Esther, you know I love you as my own daughter. I want to be sure you will be well taken care of, and that means I need to find you a husband."

"Uncle, are you sick? Is that what you're trying to tell me? I mean, I know your nightmares have gotten worse lately—"

Mordecai waved his hand, dismissing that.

"Oh, no, daughter, I'm fine, it's not that. Thank you, but I really am well. I just think it's time for you to marry and start your own life."

"Wow, why is everyone talking to me about marriage today? Leenah said the same thing."

"We're both right then. Leenah and I both know it's time."

Esther was quiet for a while. She was afraid of where her thoughts might take her.

"Uncle, when I think about marriage, I have a blank in my mind. Grandma and Grandpa and Mom and Dad were dead before I could remember them. I have no model for marriage. When I try to think about what I would want in marriage, I imagine being able to tell my husband everything in my heart and mind, like I do with God. But I know that can't be."

"Right. It's against the rules."

"But if a man loves me, shouldn't he love the real me?"

"Esther, I'm afraid it's just not that simple."

"Why can't it be? Why can't we return to a simpler time like how Adam and Eve were in the Garden together with God?"

"What happened next, Esther! Within just a few generations, Adam and Eve's children were raping and killing each other! That's why God sent the Flood to put an end to that! We can't go back to that time. We can only do the best we can with where we are right now, at least until Messiah comes!"

Esther looked down at the floor, studying it. Suddenly, there was a pounding knock on the door.

"Open up! Open up! By order of the king!"

Mordecai ran to the door and obeyed immediately, true to the rules: "Obey right away especially with authority." There were palace soldiers standing there, armed.

Mordecai froze. Armed soldiers at the doorstep once again! Was this history repeating itself! Would these men kill him and his precious niece! Nooooo, please, God, no!

The soldier on the right spoke first.

"King Xerxes has become displeased with Queen Vashti and has put her away. He now seeks a new queen for his kingdom. All young virgins are being summoned to the harem, and he will choose the most beautiful to be his queen."

The second soldier opened a scroll and looked at it.

"According to our kingdom records, there is a young unmarried woman living here. Goes by the name of Esther."

He saw and beckoned to Esther who was standing behind her uncle in fear.

Mordecai was torn. He was too late! The rules said he had to obey and hand Esther over, but how could he send her off to marry a foreign king! Was this what his dream had been warning him of!

"No, Uncle, I can't leave you!" Esther ran to the back of the room, Mordecai following her.

"Daughter, you know the rules! We must obey! Please, don't make this harder than it is! The order has been given, and we must comply! Go with these men, and I will be outside the court of the women every day to check on you. Being the wife of a king is a great honor. Maybe this is for the best or even what God has planned for you! And even if not, remember, God is always with us, a sure help in times of trouble. Now go! Don't make the men wait! I love you, daughter!"

Mordecai hugged Esther and pushed her toward the door. Swallowing her tears, she looked back one last time as the men tore her away.

And then she was gone.

CHAPTER 4

Entering the Harem

A short and uncomfortable bumpy carriage ride through the streets took Esther to the court of the women, King Xerxes's harem. When the door of the carriage opened, a man was there.

"Welcome, lady. I am Hegai, head eunuch and keeper of the women. Follow me."

It was if she could hear Mordecai's voice in her head: "Obey, daughter, obey!"

She followed Hegai down a long hallway. Esther had never seen so many bright colors! Gorgeous tapestries lined the walls, all of them shiny and luxurious. It smelled so good in there too, like perfume and spices. Esther was overwhelmed! At the end of the hallway, it opened up to a large room full of women who were all chattering excitedly. Hegai tapped Esther's shoulder.

"Listen up, girl, since you'll find I don't like to repeat myself. To your right is the kitchen. You girls will be getting special meals for your figure to be perfect. To the left is the beauty salon where you'll be getting all the fancy treatments: nails, hair, makeup, waxing, perfume, everything. You want to look your best when you go see the king. Down the hall to the right is your sleeping quarters. By quick assessment of looking at you, you won't need many treatments. You're already pretty and have a great figure. In fact, I'd say you can go to the king tomorrow for your turn. Any questions?"

Esther's head was spinning, but she really had only one question. "What about Vashti? Where is she?"

Hegai looked confused. "Really? That's your question? You should be more concerned about learning the ropes here, not about the woman you might be replacing."

"The soldiers said the king was displeased with Vashti. Shouldn't I talk to her to find out how to not displease him?"

Hegai's look softened. Now it was Esther's turn to be confused. One second ago, this man had a look of cold ice. Now he looked kind. He drew near her and lowered his voice.

"Listen, girl, I need to put on a tough face since most girls here need it to whip them into shape. But you're different, I can tell. You actually care about Vashti, asked about her, the poor dear. Plus, you're smart. Instead of being self-absorbed like many girls here, you're looking ahead to the future and looking to do your research so you can truly please the king. Well done! I'm impressed. Tell you what. I'll take you to Vashti, and then I'll take you to a private room for yourself. You don't have to sleep in the common quarters with the others. I like you. You've won my favor. Now, follow me. I'll take you to Vashti's room."

Esther gratefully followed as Hegai proceeded toward the hallway. As they walked by the "common quarters," Esther thought to herself it was very luxurious indeed, hardly what she'd call common! Fluffy pillows everywhere, several soft couches, fancy carpets, and everything was so colorful!

Hegai stopped after a short walk down the hallway and knocked on what must be Vashti's door.

"Vashti? You have a visitor. May we come in?"

"Why not? Why does it matter anyway?"

Hegai sighed. "Good enough, I guess." He pushed the door open.

Vashti was lying on her bed, sitting up as Hegai and Esther came in.

Vashti was beautiful. Tall and slender, with tan skin, long, wavy dark-red hair, and green eyes. She stared at Esther suspiciously.

"And who, may I ask, are you?"

Esther bowed her head in respect. "My queen!"

Vashti scoffed. "Not anymore. Well, I guess technically not until the next queen is chosen would I officially not be queen anymore. You didn't answer my question, girl."

"My name is Esther. I just got here and asked to see you. I wanted to know how it was you displeased the king, so I can avoid doing the same."

Vashti rose from the bed in fury. "So you think you're better than me? You literally just got here, and you think you can do better!"

Esther knew, when she spoke her mind, it didn't always go well, and this was just one example. "No, no, I'm so sorry. I didn't mean to offend my queen. I just need to know what happened. I want to do my best."

"Well, what a conscientious little man pleaser we have on our hands, now don't we, Hegai? I'll give you the short version. That man wanted me at his beck and call! I was having a banquet with my ladies here, and he called me to his own banquet and then had the nerve to get upset when I didn't show. Ha! Now, get out, and don't use any more of my precious time! I want to really enjoy these last few days as queen."

Hegai put his hands around Esther's shoulders. "Let's go, dear. Time to go to your room."

Vashti slammed the door behind them.

Esther took a deep breath. Hegai looked at her with sympathy.

"It's hard seeing her. I'm sorry but you did ask to, and first thing. Please don't take it personally. She's taking it really hard."

"Thanks for that. Now I have something to think about to make myself ready for tomorrow."

"You're welcome. Now, follow me to your room."

Esther followed and Hegai opened the door, letting her in. Esther gasped. It was almost as nice as Vashti's room!

"You'll be comfortable here. Now, rest up Esther. There's a long day to prepare tomorrow. Any other questions?"

Esther shook her head.

He nodded. And with that, Hegai was gone.

Esther lay down on the bed, exhausted. Her heart hadn't stopped pounding since the soldiers had arrived at the door back at home. *Well, I guess this is my new home now?*

True to habit, Esther prayed in her head. *God, thank You that I am safe. Thank You that it seems I have a confidante in Hegai. Thank You for the comfort of this beautiful room and the privileged information I got from Vashti. Lord, it sounds like Vashti disrespected the king, and he has put her away from him, like King David did with his first wife Michal since she despised him in her heart, making sure she was taken care of, but not going to her ever again. God, please continue to protect me and direct my path. Whatever Your will is, whatever has brought me here, let me please You. And if it also be Your will, let me please the king. Watch over Mordecai. I'll see him tomorrow outside the court of women. Thank You, God, for hearing my prayer and for being with me always. Amen.*

CHAPTER 5

Making Herself Ready

When Esther woke up, she couldn't remember where she was. Then it all came rushing back to her. She sat up, determined to do her best to please the king and to honor God.

Breakfast was an elaborate meal of fruit and milkshakes of different flavors. After eating, ladies from the salon escorted her back to her room for her wedding-night bath. They filled the basin with warm water and shaved and waxed her so all her skin was perfectly soft. When she dried off, they rubbed oils and perfumes on her, making her smell as fragrant as the harem when she'd arrived! The bath made Esther's curls even more full and lively, cascading down her back. As the finishing touch, they dressed her in a white gown. Next, the salon. The women curled her hair till the curls shined like gold and bounced with effortless softness. Esther knew her body looked presentable, but had she prepared her mind and heart?

"May I see the other wives today before I go to the king?" she asked the ladies doing her makeup.

"Girl, as long as you don't mess up all our work on you, do whatever you want."

Esther chuckled.

"Outside the salon is the common room. You can stay there till it's your time. Many girls come in and out of there during the day. Just a few are Xerxes's wives. Most of the women living here in the harem are servant girls, chefs, and those who work in the salon, like me. Yesterday, nine more girls were brought in from the surrounding citadel of Susa, you included. Mingle all you want."

Esther nodded gratefully. When she was finally ready to leave the salon, she proceeded to the common room. Hegai was there with seven young girls.

"Good evening, Esther. These are your seven maidens I've provided you. They can help you with whatever you need."

Esther was shocked! What more could she want or need, never mind seven maids to help her with it!

"Thank you, Hegai. I just want to stay here and get to know some ladies before it's my turn."

Nodding, Hegai walked away. Esther sat down.

"Hello. I just want to learn as much as I can about this place."

"What do you want to know? My name is Zarine."

"Hi, Zarine. I guess I want to do more research about the king's wives. Where are they, and where are all the king's children?"

A second maid spoke. "I'm Mirabella. He has seven wives, well, now six since he and Vashti aren't together anymore. He has five children and one on the way. The children live in separate private quarters with their mothers between the harem and the rest of the palace."

"I'd really like to meet the king's children some other time, but could you please take me to the girl who is carrying his child right now?"

"Sure." Mirabella took her hand and led her down the hall to the bathroom.

"Why are we going this way?"

The girls giggled. Zarine answered, "Nine times out of ten, that's where she is. She's very close to giving birth, so she has to pee all the time!"

Sure enough, as soon as they got to the bathroom, a very pregnant girl came out, waddling.

"Hi. I'm Esther."

"Hello. Serapina. Very pregnant Serapina."

The girls laughed and walked back to the common room. Serapina spoke again.

"So, Esther, I see you're all dolled up. It's your wedding night with the king tonight, right?"

"Yes."

"Well, us girls need to help each other out. I'm guessing you want some information about our husband, yes?"

"What do I need to know?"

"Honestly, my wedding night was so long ago, I don't remember at all. I'm sorry I can't be of more help. But if you have any pregnancy questions, I have so much to say!"

"Thanks, Serapina. But I'm not there yet. I guess just wish me luck?"

"Of course. Well, back to the bathroom I go. Pregnancy sure is uncomfortable!"

Esther watched Serapina walk away, saying a silent prayer for her. *God, please watch over her and the king's child she carries. I pray for a safe birth and a healthy child. Amen.*

Zarine spoke up. "Where to now, Esther? It's almost time for you to go in to see the king!"

Esther was nervous. These maid girls were so very young and innocent. They seemed happy and excited for her, but what did they possibly know, really? Did they even really know what happened on a wedding night? They were acting so happy for Esther. Should she be happy? What even is happiness, she wondered. What did she know about this king anyway? He was a total stranger to her, and she was about to marry him. Would he even be kind to her? She had tried to get answers from the one other wife she'd met, Serapina, but was afraid to ask what she really needed to: would she be safe with him?

"I need to talk to my uncle. He's waiting for me outside. But I can go alone. He raised me, so it's like my father giving me away before I get married. Something like that anyway."

The maidens nodded and returned to their places to talk to the others.

Esther headed outside. Time to see Mordecai.

CHAPTER 6

Father of the Bride

The sun was setting. This day had gone by so quickly! Almost night-time already, her wedding night with the king was fast approaching. Esther's stomach was in knots. But she couldn't think about that right now. Her uncle must have been waiting for her all day, and she shouldn't keep him waiting and worrying any longer.

Esther's heart hurt when she saw Mordecai waiting for her outside the gate. Of course, he was there, just as he said he would be. She ran to him and held out her hand, poking it through the gate bars and grabbing onto his shoulder. She could tell he had been crying from his tear-stained face and his squeaky voice when he spoke.

"Esther, you look so pretty. The king will surely be pleased with you. We don't really know anything about him, so just in case he has a temper, it's good you please him. You know your safety is my main priority."

"Uncle, remember you wanted to find me a husband? Well, God has provided one." Esther was putting on a brave face, partly for her uncle and partly for her own sake.

Mordecai was tearing up again. "God knows this isn't how I pictured your wedding day, daughter. I love you. Be brave. Be strong. Have faith."

He placed his hand through the bars and onto her shoulder. "Yahweh, bless my daughter, and watch over her. Keep her safe. Amen."

Esther couldn't speak. She nodded, smiled, and turned around. It was time to see the king.

Walking back, Hegai met her. "Happy wedding day, dear one. How are you feeling?"

Esther wiped away tears.

"That good then?"

Esther laughed. "Thanks, Hegai. I needed that. Just pretty emotional saying goodbye to my uncle. He's basically my father. He's the one who brought me up. I didn't really get to say goodbye last night since the soldiers arrived suddenly, and now I'm here."

"Right. I get it. Not easy. I hope you got the information you wanted from Serapina. You're a smart girl, Esther. You'll be fine. Really. Like I said when you first arrived, I can tell you're different from the others. But in a good way. If he likes his other wives, he will surely be quite pleased with you."

Esther wished she believed it. As she walked with Hegai back inside and through the harem, she looked around at the other girls. They all seemed so happy. Esther wondered what that was like. *God, can I be happy someday?* She'd been raised to view safety as the unattainable goal to focus on. It wasn't easy to enjoy life when you were always fighting to feel safe.

Exiting the harem, they passed through to another long hallway. Next came a silver winding stairwell and another hallway. The last door at the end must have been the bridal chamber since Hegai stopped there. This whole long walk, Esther had continued praying, even though she couldn't think of any words. They had reached the door now. Time was up.

"Good luck, Esther." Hegai opened the door.

Esther walked in, and Hegai closed the door behind her, making Esther think of when God shut the door of Noah's ark. Would she be safe in here as God had protected Noah and his family?

She was about to find out.

CHAPTER 7

One Night with the King

The room was splendid. What a bridal chamber! Roses everywhere, an elaborate feast spread out on the table, and of course, a huge golden bed. Esther tried not to look at that.

By the table stood a man. The king of course. He was quite tall and very dark. His hair was coarse, a mass of fuzzy, black curls. He turned around and looked at her. She found him to be extremely handsome.

"Hi. Thanks for coming. Please, have a seat."

Esther was surprised. The king was pleasantly polite. Esther sat down at the table as the king also did.

"Please, help yourself to whatever you'd like."

"Thank you." She wasn't that hungry, but she took some pineapple, figs, and olives and put them on her plate. The king stared at her. She glanced up at him.

"I'm sorry to stare, it's just… Well, forgive me for stating the obvious, but you're so beautiful. I'm just wondering how it is you hadn't married yet. What is your age?"

"I'm nineteen, your Majesty."

"Please. Call me Xerxes."

"Okay. To answer your question about marriage, I guess I was waiting for something."

"Waiting for something? Like what? Love?"

Esther was caught off guard. What a thing to ask! Such a personal question!

"Okay, let's level the playing field. I asked you questions, but you should also be able to ask me. Go ahead."

First, he was polite, then he asked intrusive questions, then he decided to be fair about it. She couldn't figure this man out. But for whatever reason, she was starting to feel less nervous and more comfortable around him. It felt like what Mordecai always wanted for her, safety. Is this what it feels like to be safe?

"What is your age?"

"Thirty-five."

How well did he know his family? She would test him and see if his answers matched what her maids had told her.

"How many children do you have?"

"Five so far. My wives have been fertile. I've only been king a few years. I have another child on the way."

Good. His answers were lining up.

"Right. Serapina."

He looked impressed.

"You met her? I see you've taken an interest in this family already. You're off to a good start. Um, I'm sorry what is your name?"

Esther laughed. "It's all right. I know you have a few wives to keep track of." What was it about this man that made her even more open than usual? "My name is Esther. It means myrtle tree."

"That's really lovely. How is Serapina doing?"

It was nice how he asked about his pregnant wife. That was reassuring.

"She's uncomfortable."

He laughed. "That's pregnancy for you! I'll have to send for her so she can visit me soon. What other questions do you have for me?"

"Xerxes, can you please tell me how this works? If you're not pleased with me, what happens?"

"As soon as you came into this palace, you legally became my wife. I'm a man who takes care of his own. You are part of this family and will be taken care of here, forever. That goes for any child you give me too."

Suddenly, Esther became nervous again when he mentioned children. She looked away.

"Don't worry, Esther, it's all right. When it is time for that, I don't force you. That's not me. I don't know what people think about me, but I'm not an animal. A man never forces his woman. Furthermore, I promise I will tend to your needs."

Esther nodded, relieved and deeply moved by his words.

"Right. Thank you. I can see you are a very good man. I'm so sorry it didn't work out for you with your first queen. Can you please tell me about what happened with Vashti?"

His face changed, and he looked distressed, shifting in his seat.

"I'm sorry, I don't want to bring you pain! It's just I feel I should hear from you what happened, especially since I'm your wife now."

"You're right. You're absolutely right, Esther. Thank you for asking. This is embarrassing for me, but I will tell you the truth. Remember how you said you were waiting for something with marriage? Same here. If I simply wanted to have many children, I would just have my wives. My advisors say having a queen is a political thing, but for me, I wanted my queen wife to be someone special. A woman I could really be myself with. You see, Esther, out there, I'm the king. With my queen, I would want to be just me, Xerxes. It saddens me that I've never found this. My wives are all on some level afraid of me, and I don't know why. Either that or they just obey me, coming to visit me when I send for them, but they don't give me their heart. With Vashti, I thought I had found someone special because she didn't seem to fear me. But the day she refused to come to the banquet I made for her, well, that was the day I realized she did feel something different for me, but it wasn't a good thing. She feels disdain for me. It just hurt so much because I tried to open my heart to her, and she shut me out. It isn't easy for a man to admit something like that."

"Why should it embarrass you to share what happened? I'm sorry she hurt you."

"You're kind, Esther. You're very kind. Thank you."

Esther decided to take a risk. She wouldn't reveal her Jewish identity, but she would try to find out his views about her people.

"How do you feel about Jews?"

"Interesting question. I have no opinion, really. I know many have something against them, but I see no problem with Jews. They are people like anyone else. My grandfather, King Cyrus, freed the Hebrew captives and let them go back to Israel. I wish to follow his legacy in maintaining as much peace as possible for my kingdom. I'm sure many Jews remain here since, surely, not all of them returned to Israel after Cyrus's decree. But tell me, Esther, why are you asking me about politics? Tonight isn't about that."

"Aren't you interviewing me to be queen? How is that not political?"

Xerxes grinned. He had a beautiful smile, and dimples too, Esther noticed.

"Esther, I can see you're not afraid of me, are you? That's good, that's really good. And yes, as I said, my advisors tell me having a queen wife is good for politics, but as I said, I consider it more a matter of the heart. I haven't found my true queen yet. I'm still searching, and I really hope to find her."

They continued eating. Neither one had any more questions. At the end of the meal, Xerxes stood up and held out his hand to her. She placed her hand in his, a little apprehensive, but mostly calm. Together, they walked over to the bed.

This is it.

God, be with me.

CHAPTER 8

Decision Day

The next morning, Esther gradually woke up, keeping her eyes closed as she reflected. She had never slept so well in her life or had such a peaceful morning! Esther was used to waking up to Uncle Mordecai's nightmare screams, the poor man. Even yesterday, she had woken up from her own anxiety dreams about meeting the king. This morning was completely different. Esther knew why, of course. It was because of what had happened the night before with Xerxes.

When he'd begun to embrace and kiss her, at first, she had felt strange, even scared. But that had quickly disappeared. Before she knew it, she was kissing and embracing him right back with the same passion! Nothing wrong with it. He was her husband after all, and he had already shown himself to be kind. He was so attractive, in both face and physique! Eyes and skin like dark chocolate with muscle definition throughout his whole body! She soon experienced just how strong Xerxes was! So unbelievably strong! Everything that happened between them had just seemed so natural, and when they were finished, they simply fell asleep.

God, I know Uncle Mordecai was right. We can't go back to the Garden time of Adam and Eve. But now, I know You made it to be such a nice experience, man and wife coming together as one flesh. Thank You, God, for this gift!

Miraculously, she not only felt safe. She felt…happy? *Is this happiness? What a wonder!*

Smiling, Esther finally opened her eyes. She was surprised to see Xerxes sitting on the edge of the bed by her side, fully clothed, and looking down at her. She figured he'd have been long gone by then! Busy life of a king he must have. But no. He was still there with her.

Suddenly she felt self-conscious. The wedding night was over, and Xerxes was back in his clothes while she was still naked under the sheet! She pulled it up over her body to cover herself completely.

Another grin from Xerxes.

"No need to hide from me, Esther. You really are so beautiful. And I'm sorry, I didn't want to startle you. I just liked watching you sleep. I found it very soothing."

True to form, Esther said what she was thinking.

"Right. I bet you say that to all your wives."

Xerxes laughed. "You have a response for everything, don't you? And no, actually, I don't. In fact, this is the first time I…well, anyway." Xerxes stood up awkwardly and then turned around to face her. "Listen, Esther, I'll get right to the point. I've decided to make you queen."

Esther's jaw dropped. She couldn't believe it! She sat up, causing the sheet to fall, then snatched it up to cover herself once more.

"Xerxes, that's a really big decision choosing your queen! Don't you want to sleep on it first!"

Xerxes narrowed his eyes and cocked his head to the side, looking amused and annoyed at the same time.

"Esther. I don't want to be crass, but I just slept with you. How is that not sleeping on it?"

The blood rushed to Esther's cheeks.

Xerxes sat down on the bed next to her and took a deep breath.

"What I mean is, I already know all I need to know to make this decision."

"How! How do you know this is the right decision! How do you know I'm the one for this!"

"That! That, right there! That's it, Esther! You're not afraid to talk to me and ask me questions. I really like that! And I can be myself with you. I know we're still getting to know each other, and we just met, but that's all I need to know for now. Most people, especially my wives, act afraid of me or treat me like I'm either too dangerous or too fragile. It's exhausting being king. I see in you a true partner. I feel really good and open with you, and that means the world to me. A king cannot trust everyone, but I want to trust my queen wife. And I love how comfortable you are with me. It's not just about talking and trust either. Feelings matter too. It's pretty clear we feel the same way about each other based on how you returned my affections in bed."

Esther nodded. Definitely a very powerful mutual attraction.

Xerxes was quite an intelligent man. He'd thought this through, and everything he said was making sense. Still, did all that really mean she was ready to be the queen of Persia?

"Thanks for being so kind to me. And for not taking my questions the wrong way. And about last night, thank you for treating me so well. I was nervous, but then I wasn't. I felt safe in your arms, and I don't have a lot of experience feeling safe in my life."

"That's really sad, Esther. I hope you always feel safe with me because you are safe with me. I will always protect you. You're my wife, and more than that, I'm making you my queen. You will always be safe with me. I promise you that. I want everyone in my family to be safe, and more than that, everyone in my kingdom too."

Esther smiled. It sounded a lot like what God promised for when the Messiah would come. Security and peace for all. *Thank You, God, for this blessing! Maybe I really am safe with this man?*

Xerxes looked toward the door. Esther could see the anxiety on his face.

"When I walk out that door, I'm king again. It was really nice just being Xerxes with you last night, Esther. Thank you."

Esther felt for him. Suddenly, she longed to hug him but felt that would be inappropriate. It was one thing to embrace the man last night while he was taking her as his wife. It was another to do so in the light of day, entirely on her own. She stayed still.

Xerxes stood up again.

"You can stay here as long as you wish today. Tonight, you will be expected back at the court of women. Tomorrow will be the coronation ceremony to make you queen. I'll be in meetings with advisors all day today, and then tonight, planning for the ceremony. I'll see you tomorrow, and I will miss you until then."

He leaned down to kiss her forehead.

"Have a good day, Esther."

Then he was gone.

CHAPTER 9

Xerxes Reflects and Shares the News

Putting on his king face, Xerxes walked down the hallway in the direction of the meeting room. Indeed, it had been difficult to leave his new bride, but now it was time to make his announcement to his advisors. He dreaded their reactions. No doubt, they'd think him insane for choosing so quickly. But it didn't matter. He felt more than confident in his decision.

He found his thoughts turning back to Esther even as he walked farther away from her. Esther was the eighth woman he'd been with, as he'd taken seven wives during his time as king, Vashti included. Apparently, eighth time was the charm in terms of finding the right woman for him! And what a woman she was! Such a sweet girl in every sense of the word! Of course, as soon as he saw her, he'd been more than taken with her beautiful face. Not to mention that body of hers! What a sight to behold! Truly, he'd never seen such a stunning woman in all his life. Yet she was even more charming and refreshing when she opened her mouth to speak to him. What a nice change of pace for someone to address him as a human being, not as someone to be feared! He hadn't known it was possible for someone to see him that way, never mind a new wife. But Esther was clearly different. She wasn't afraid and spoke kindly to him. She carried herself with royalty yet humility. What a queen he had found!

What was it about this girl that made him share so much? He'd confided in Esther things he hadn't shared with any living soul, his search for a queen and why, and the truth about why Vashti was no longer his queen. The kingdom had been told she had displeased him as a cover story for politics and saving face, per the guidance of his advisors. But the truth was, he had been disillusioned to find his quest for love had ended abruptly when he chose the wrong queen. Of course, he couldn't admit the true story to anyone, but for whatever reason, he had poured out his heart easily to Esther. It felt so good to share the secrets of his heart with her!

Xerxes wasn't naive. He knew many men envied his marital life, thinking it a fantasy world to choose one woman from a handful of wives any night. Fools! Little did they know, the reality was far from glamorous. As he had explained to Esther, his wives seemed afraid or distant toward him. This was especially true on the wedding night, when it was a wife's first time. No matter how caring and gentle he tried to be, no wife had ever truly engaged with him. It seemed clear to Xerxes that a man should not feel alone while in the conjugal act. Yet as ironic and pathetic as it was, that was exactly how he had always felt, alone in his marriage bed. It had always been the same, every time, with every wife, ever since Xerxes' own first time with the first wife he'd taken. But not so last night with Esther! No, not at all!

Xerxes felt his king face fade away as he broke out in a wide grin, thinking back on the previous night. She had followed his lead surprisingly quickly and naturally, kissing and embracing him with such enthusiastic sincerity that it had brought tears to his eyes! Xerxes had never felt so wanted! Such a gorgeous woman, with long black curls, caramel skin, and eyes like honey. The way she had gazed upon his face and body with those eyes when he had taken off his clothes made him feel so alive! And when she took off her clothes, Xerxes was barely able to stand it. Breathtaking! Esther was adorably petite in stature and totally voluptuous in form. She was simply perfect! Taking her in his arms just felt so right! That was where she belonged! And what about her delightful little squeals and later screams of pleasure? Absolutely intoxicating to his ears! How glad he was to know Esther had enjoyed herself as much as he had last night! Such a remarkable young woman deserved all that and more!

Xerxes had fallen asleep afterward, and he had slept very well. This was not typical given the amount of anxiety he carried as king. But last night, he had been able to be just himself, just a man with his new wife, and a totally new experience with this woman.

Did Esther even know how amazing she was? No! She didn't! And that was one of her best qualities. She was unassuming and humble, not pretentious in the least. What a wonderful queen she would be!

Obviously, he was both fascinated and infatuated with Esther. Deep down, Xerxes had always wished to find something resembling, well, love. Meeting this enchanting new wife had resurrected that dream. Could he and Esther truly fall in love? He would only know for sure when more time had passed, but he felt hopeful. Now was not the time to keep thinking on these things. He was almost at the end of the hallway.

Xerxes put his king face back on, took a deep breath, and opened the door to the meeting room. Just as he'd expected, the room was full and noisy, the men clearly wondering where he'd been. Karshena spoke first.

"Where have you been, Your Majesty? We've all been waiting and worrying."

Xerxes smiled and sat down, taking his seat at the head of the table.

"And good morning to you too! Well, if you all must know, I was waiting for my new wife to wake up so I could speak to her."

"Speak to her?" Shethar asked, incredulous. "What for? Don't tell me you chose her? Already?"

Nodding, Xerxes spoke again. "Yes. That is what I was speaking to her about. She will be my queen. Her name is Esther."

"And what about the other maidens, Your Majesty?" Admatha asked. "We brought in nine young ladies from the surrounding cit-adel to possibly be queen, and instead you picked the very first one. Should we send the rest of the maidens back to their homes?"

"Yes, send them back, I say," Shethar agreed. "Why keep them here? The palace can't be burdened with extra people to care for, not to mention the cost."

Karshena spoke next with a suggestion. "Your Majesty, if I may, let's send them to the streets to be prostitutes. Their mothers must have forgotten them by now, and they are surely quite pretty. They would serve the kingdom well that way."

Xerxes glared at him. "Karshena, you know I've never much cared for your sense of humor, but whether you're joking right now or not, I will answer you. No! Absolutely not! Just in case anyone here needs a reminder, prostitution is against the law in my kingdom. No woman should ever feel she has to sell herself. That is vile and appalling! Are we clear, everybody?"

The men nodded. Xerxes continued. "As for your original question, Admatha, I will get back to that now. These maidens who have come into the palace are all legally my wives now, and I will take care of them. And regarding cost to the palace, that is not an issue at all. You are being stingy as always. We have plenty of money. I am well up to date on our financial records as always. In fact, there's of course enough for the ceremony and banquet for Esther's coronation tomorrow. Of course we can take care of these nine maidens brought in. Anyway, if you wish to be political about it, as I know you all do, think of it this way: Women make up a huge part of the population in the kingdom. It's clearly not in my best interest to treat them poorly by sending them back once they were told they would be a king's wife. Furthermore, these maidens shouldn't be penalized just because I happened to find my queen with the first one Hegai sent me."

"Your Majesty, you've always been so idealistic with your policies. On the one hand, I admire it, on the other I think you take it too far at times. Like with Vashti, you really should have killed her after she disrespected you so." Karshena shook his head after speaking.

"This coming from the man who a minute ago suggested we send them out to be prostitutes? Yes, I'm sure my views seem 'too far at times' for you. But to me, this is the right way. And about Vashti, she's still my wife in the sense that I promised to care for her when she came to the palace, just like the others. I know she has rejected me and I accept that, but I refuse to penalize or punish her, much less kill her. We've already discussed all this. Regarding the new wives, make sure the proper bride price is given to each of their families. Esther's family should, of course, receive three times that amount, as she will be the queen wife. I also have some messages for you to send to Hegai today please. Now that I have nine new wives, including Esther, I want to make a schedule to be sure I will be treating them all fairly. Esther and I will be taking political tours around the kingdom together, but we'll never be gone more than a week so I won't neglect my other wives. Since Vashti and I aren't in a relationship anymore, my remaining six wives, and now the nine new ones makes fifteen. Tell Hegai the following please: I wish for him to send Esther to me every other night. That leaves fifteen days each month for my other wives. Each of those nights he can send me another wife from the other fourteen. It's important that I have time devoted to being with each of them, and so they can receive their conjugal rights as wives. As for tonight, tell Hegai I wish to see Serapina. Esther told me she's not been feeling well, and so I want to comfort her."

Shethar spoke up, furrowing his brow with worry.

"I'm sorry, Your Majesty, but I'm concerned. You just met this girl, and she's already giving you orders? Are you sure we don't have another Vashti on our hands? Why did you choose her, if we may ask?"

Xerxes looked into the distance, breathing deeply to keep calm. These men could be so condescending and judgmental at times!

"Gentlemen, that is not what happened. Esther did not give me an order. She provided me with valuable information about a member of our family, one of my wives. She did so because she really cares about our family, just like I do. I used that information to make a decision about which wife I should spend tonight with. As for Esther, I feel I can trust her. I know I can. And she's not like Vashti. Don't worry, I know I'm not making the same mistake twice. I trust her, and I'm asking you to trust my judgment."

They nodded, and Admatha spoke. "Very well then, your Majesty. We'll spread the news across the kingdom, right away."

Xerxes nodded, and they continued with the meeting.

CHAPTER 10

Preparing to Be Queen

Esther stayed in the bed for a while, collecting her thoughts. This was so much to take in! She had just come to the palace, gotten married, and lost her virginity to Xerxes. Not only that, but he had immediately chosen her to be queen, and that was to happen tomorrow!

It was clear God had protected her and she was thankful. But did God approve of her marriage? After all, Xerxes didn't believe in her God. And what about Xerxes? Didn't the man deserve to know who he'd just married, slept with, and chosen as his queen? Uncle Mordecai had always taught her to keep her Jewish identity secret to keep her safe, but she still felt a husband should know his wife's heart. Especially when Xerxes himself had expressed such a yearning for closeness with her. Did God require her to share this with her husband? Did Xerxes truly want to know her origins? So many questions!

When she finally rose from the bed, she gathered up the sheet with her virgin blood. The law of Moses passed down among her people said to keep it in case the husband later turned against her and said she hadn't been a virgin when they came together. But she saw no reason for this. Xerxes seemed to be a very good man, and he'd explained that she was his wife and family forever since coming to the palace. Even Vashti, who had clearly hurt him beyond words, would stay in the harem forever and be safe and provided for all her days, just never go to him again. Indeed, Xerxes was kind and fair. No reason to hold onto her virgin blood. She put it to wash. *Thank You, God, for giving me a good man for a husband, even in a foreign land!*

Esther had to laugh when she saw herself in the mirror. Her hair and makeup were in total disarray, evidence of the passionate night she'd shared with Xerxes. She looked like an unkempt clown! Yet that morning when he looked upon her, the man had said she was beautiful. Truly he was sweet and gentlemanly, and he seemed to really like her. Esther liked him quite a bit too. After she bathed and dressed, Esther began walking back to the court of women. Thankfully, she somehow remembered the way down the hallway, winding staircase, and another hallway. Yesterday, when she had walked this same path, she had been so nervous, she could barely think. *Thank You, God, for directing my steps when I'm nervous, and when I'm not! Thank You for always being with me!*

As she approached the harem doorway, she reflected a bit. She had left this harem a fearful virgin and was returning as a relieved, newlywed wife. Her husband was a good man and had treated her well! Thanks be to God! She gathered herself to hold her happiness in her heart. Would she be able to keep this sense of peace, or would it be taken from her again?

Taking a deep breath, she opened the door to enter the harem. Inside, it was absolute chaos! The women all gathered around her, talking a mile a minute. The news about her being chosen as queen had evidently already spread throughout the palace.

Vashti approached.

"Well, if it isn't the little man charmer herself! What did you do to him! How is it he chose you, just like that?"

Esther again felt the blood rush to her cheeks.

"Nothing! I didn't do anything!"

Vashti laughed. "Are you saying you two didn't—"

Esther looked away. Those moments were private, just between her and Xerxes. "It doesn't seem right to talk about it."

"Aha! I knew it! You put a spell on him, didn't you!"

This Vashti was relentless!

"No spells, ever! That's not even—" Esther stopped herself midsentence. Her people didn't believe in spells. Only God has true power. All power comes from God. But she couldn't say that out loud and risk anyone finding out she was Jewish. She only hoped she could share her true self with Xerxes someday, but only time would tell. He said she was safe with him and promised to protect her, always. Would he? She could only hope at this point.

Suddenly, Esther noticed Hegai making his way toward her.

"Congratulations, Esther!" He then looked at Vashti. "As for you, Vashti, we all know you're sad about not being queen anymore, but that's no reason to treat Esther badly. She didn't do anything to you, and she will be our queen soon. She deserves our respect."

Touched, Esther mouthed the words "Thank you" then went to her room to continue in thought and prayer. Time to get ready for tomorrow, coronation day. She smiled at the thought of seeing Xerxes again with his reassuring and warm grin.

CHAPTER 11

Another Father

Entering her room, Esther plopped down in her bed and took a deep breath.

There came a knock at the door. Who could it be?

"Esther, it's Hegai. May I come in please?"

Esther sat up. Hegai was a nice man. No reason to be afraid of criticism from him.

"Yes, of course, Hegai."

He opened the door and came to sit on a chair next to the bed.

"Once again, I must apologize for how Vashti's treated you. She's taken it really hard about being deposed, but like I said, you didn't do anything to her, and she shouldn't treat you poorly. I'm so sorry, Esther."

She smiled. "Thanks. I know. Thanks for caring."

"Of course, I care! To me, you girls are all my daughters. I'm a eunuch. Of course, I can't have a family like other men. But this is my family. You all are my family. Everyone has a place in the royal family, and in the kingdom, and this is mine, and I'm thankful."

"That's beautiful, Hegai."

"So are you, my dear. And tomorrow, you'll not only be my newest daughter, you'll be my queen! How are you feeling about it?"

"So overwhelmed! I don't know the first thing about being a queen!"

"Ha! No matter. As I said, I knew you were different as soon as you got here. Way different from the others. You were the last to arrive the other day, but I knew you should go to the king first. Trust me, you have what it takes to be his queen. Anyway, the king clearly is happy with you, and I can tell from your face, you're happy with him too, right?"

Esther nodded, smiling.

"This morning, before he left the room, he told me he would miss me till tomorrow at the ceremony. And I definitely miss him already too."

"Esther, that's amazing! That means the two of you are beginning to fall in love!"

"Really?"

"Yes, of course! I still remember how that felt, even though it was many years ago when I was a young man before I was made a eunuch. You miss the person, want to be with them and talk to them more, think about them a lot…"

Esther nodded, vigorously.

"See? I told you! This is wonderful news, my dear! This will be so good for our family, and the kingdom too, for our king and queen to truly love each other. As much as Vashti means to us, I knew she wasn't the one for the king. It's you, Esther. You have come to bring light to the kingdom, I can tell!"

"Everyone seems to think I can do this but me. Thanks for believing in me, Hegai."

"You just need to believe in yourself, Esther. You already won the king's favor, did you not? Now, the rest will happen in time. You'll see. You will be a lovely queen, and just what we all need. True love is more than the feeling. It's also the willingness to make sacrifices when need be for the other person. Vashti didn't understand that. She didn't want to leave her banquet, even though the king had made one for her. She wasn't able to see it from his perspective. With you, again it's so plain to see, you are different in a good way. You will be able to take risks for the king, when need be, in the future, if danger comes. And he'll do the same for you. Now, I'll let you get some rest and decompress. I know you have a big day tomorrow. Sweet dreams, daughter."

Hegai left the room.

God, You have provided me another father inside this harem. You are so generous! Thank You! Praise God from whom all blessings flow! Amen!

CHAPTER 12

Queen Esther

Sitting in the salon chair the morning of her coronation, surrounded by her seven maidens and Hegai, Esther's head was swimming again.

They fussed and fussed over her endlessly. Esther didn't hear a word they said. To her, she looked just the same as she had on the wedding night, just a different hairstyle and new jewels for her nails. What did it matter anyway? Xerxes had already chosen her and decided she'd be queen. Would the people of Persia trust her based on her beauty alone? Esther hoped not.

Now came the dress. A shiny, long, vibrant blue gown loaded with diamonds and a train that trailed behind her. Esther wondered how she would be able to walk in it!

When she was finally deemed impeccably polished by every lady's standards, Esther was escorted to the throne room. The room was crowded with so many people, all shouting. They were even louder than the harem ladies!

Xerxes came in at the front of the room, and everyone immediately became quiet. Esther saw what he meant about how people seemed afraid of him. On the one hand, it was impressive how he could change the room immediately. On the other, she knew how much this hurt him. He wanted to be beloved by his people, not feared. *God, can you help me reveal Xerxes' heart to the kingdom? How can I serve the people as his queen? What would you have me do, Lord?*

Xerxes looked different today. She was seeing him as the king right now, as opposed to just being Xerxes with her as he had said. He walked down the aisle toward her. When he reached the end, he held out his hand the same way he had invited her to the marriage bed.

Taking a deep breath, Esther placed her hand in his, and they walked together down the aisle toward the throne. Thankfully, she wasn't tripping down the aisle, and she started to feel confident walking beside her new husband in public. At the throne, Xerxes reached for a golden crown, presented it to her, and placed it on her head. Turning her to face the crowd, Xerxes raised his voice: "People of Persia, I present to you, your queen! Queen Esther, my new bride!"

"Hail, Queen Esther! Hail, Queen Esther! Hail, Queen Esther!" The people were all chanting in unison. What a sound! Esther could hardly believe her ears!

Esther smiled. She didn't know why God had raised her up to such a position of power. But she was determined to use it for good and for God's glory. Indeed, she had always hoped in the back of her mind that her future would be different. This was about as different as it could possibly be!

God, You truly are a miracle worker. Praise Yahweh!

She shifted her gaze to look at Xerxes. He was solemn, continuing with his public king persona. Still, Esther detected a tiny twinkle in his eye.

Truly, she had won the king's favor. She only hoped she could continue to honor him. She would be careful with his heart he had so tenderly offered to her, and so quickly! And in time, she hoped to show her husband her true heart as well.

God, show me the way. You have given me power. Give me wisdom as well, I pray. As Solomon, David's son, asked for wisdom to rule Israel, so I also ask to be wise as queen of Persia. Amen.

CHAPTER 13

King and Queen Together

Esther hummed happily to herself in her room as she prepared for her second night with Xerxes. What a day it had been! She was now queen of Persia! Esther couldn't believe her luck! But of course, she knew it wasn't really luck. It was a blessing from God, and God was ultimately in control of all things. Praise Him always!

When the soldiers had come to take her to the palace, she hadn't known what to think and had feared the worst would happen. Every moment between then and meeting Xerxes had been filled with trepidation, just praying for God's protection. How wrong she had been! Everything had turned out a million times better than she could have imagined!

After the ceremony, there had been a banquet in the public banquet hall. She had sat next to Xerxes, and her head had been spinning with excitement and happiness. Each time her eyes met his, she felt her heart skip a beat. She just couldn't believe what a kind man he was! Before the ceremony, Hegai had come to her room to explain the details Xerxes had specified about their marriage. He wanted to spend every other night with her and also go on political tours with her by his side! Not only that, but he would be fair to his other wives as well, sending for them one by one the other nights so they would also be able to spend time with him and have their needs met. Xerxes was showing kindness and favor to her while also being just toward the other wives. What a great man!

God, thank You! Now I see this was Your plan all along! I know You brought me to Xerxes in the bridal chamber, just like You brought Eve to Adam in the Garden! I love how You don't ever change, God! You are always working to achieve Your purpose, giving so many blessings along the way! You are so gracious and merciful! I don't know yet what the deeper meaning of my marriage and new royal status is, but I know You are behind it. Thank You, God! Xerxes is proving himself to be a righteous man toward all of us! You know I always hoped in the back of my mind for a husband who had these qualities, and You have indeed provided me with Xerxes! I feel safe with him, and I pray I will be able to keep safe his heart he has entrusted to me as queen wife. Lord, I know he has been hurt by Vashti, and I ask that I can help him. I know only You can truly heal him, but you have brought us together as helpmates for each other. Please guide me so I can help my husband. Amen!

Esther giggled as she finished getting ready. She planned to wear her coronation dress but would remove her undergarments so she would be naked underneath. The dress was made of thick material, so no one would know the difference, but it would be a nice surprise for Xerxes!

She had always imagined Eve being playful with Adam in the Garden, and she wanted to be playful with Xerxes tonight. She could tell he was insecure over Vashti's rejection and might have doubts regarding her attraction and liking toward him. She was determined to make it clear to him tonight he should have no doubts!

God, I know I can't be naked when I walk to the bridal chamber of course! Adam and Eve were naked in the Garden together. But I can do the next best thing for Xerxes, reassuring him of how I feel, that I am truly grateful for him and really with him. And being naked under my dress is the symbol of that, plus Xerxes will like it, and it will be fun! Please be with me and let me speak well to my husband tonight. In Your name, I pray!

She laughed once more as she placed her undergarments in a drawer and buttoned up her dress.

Meanwhile, Xerxes was waiting for her in the bridal chamber. He was anxious and nervous. Their first night had begun as business as usual for him with taking a wife. Talk to her, eat a meal, and make her as comfortable and happy as possible in the marriage bed. But things had been different with Esther since she'd truly connected with him, and he'd opened his heart to her and made her queen today. He was vulnerable now and doubting himself. What if he'd made a mistake? Maybe Esther had only seemed to enjoy the wedding night? Perhaps he had imagined her reaction as some sort of desperate fantasy? Maybe she had reacted to the sheer novelty of the conjugal act for her or the intensity of the experience, not really to him personally? Did she even like him at all? Was she actually attracted to him?

Come on, get it together, man! Pull yourself together! She'll be here soon, and you can't be acting a fool! Not in front of the queen! Maybe she doesn't even want to be my queen! Maybe she doesn't want me at all! Ah yes, wonderful! Now my mind's just going in circles!

Of course, at that exact moment, there was a knock on the door and Esther came in, looking brilliantly radiant as always.

Would he ever get used to seeing this girl before him?

He cleared his throat nervously.

"Esther, hi! Please come sit down at the table with me. I brought you some pineapple. You seemed to like that the other night."

He sat down, but Esther stayed where she was.

Uh-oh. Why wasn't she sitting down? Vashti had refused to come to the banquet he made her. Was Esther rejecting him now too? *Oh no…I don't think I can go through that again!*

Esther spoke then. "Don't worry, Xerxes. I will go to you, I just need to say some things first."

"Of course, Esther. You can speak freely."

"Xerxes, I want to thank you for everything you've done. I know we only met two days ago, but I already see what a very good man you are. Not just to me but to everyone. It truly is an honor for me to be your queen wife. I'm really looking forward to our life together and getting to know you better. And I know you were hurt before by your first queen. I can't heal you myself, but I am here for you. Just like you said you're here for me. I tell you the truth, and I want you to believe me when I say this: Xerxes, I really do like you. I really am with you, and I really do want you."

Xerxes had difficulty finding his voice. "Oh… Thank you, Esther. You are being so sweet and gracious with me. Thanks for speaking openly. I'm glad you continue to feel comfortable with me."

She took a step closer. "And thanks for the pineapple! You really do pay attention to what I like in all things. You are an attentive and caring husband. And I am very hungry right now, but not for food."

Xerxes was shocked! No wife had ever been so bold with him! He had never experienced being pursued! He loved this!

Esther walked to him then and put her hands on his knees. He lifted her up and onto his lap. She looked deeply into his eyes. She was so beautiful… Could this possibly be a dream? What if this wasn't real?

As if in direct response to his thoughts, Esther touched his lips then reached up and stroked his hair.

"Xerxes, can you please help me get out of this dress? I'm not wearing anything underneath."

Xerxes laughed, nodding and grinning. "Yes, of course. Whatever you need, my queen."

He drew her to him, kissing her. Esther kissed him back, just as she had done on their wedding night.

He hadn't been wrong after all! For whatever reason, this extraordinary woman seemed to truly desire him. Today he had made her queen of Persia, and tonight she was quickly becoming queen of his heart.

CHAPTER 14

Royal Life, Royal Marriage

In the next few months, Esther saw God answer her prayers a million times over.

Xerxes continued to be a caring and attentive husband to Esther and all his wives. Most days, he had huge fruit platters sent down for them with all their favorites. Pineapple for Esther and olives for Serapina. That's what she had been craving through her whole pregnancy! Soon it was time for her to give birth, and when she did, she brought forth a healthy, radiant baby girl. Esther cried when she held her in her arms! After the birth, Esther helped Serapina and her daughter move to their new quarters for Xerxes' children and their mothers.

Serapina and Esther became closer during this time after she'd given birth. It soon became evident Serapina was quite an artist, and she returned to her love of art within two months after recovering from pregnancy. Xerxes sent her personalized supplies so she could enjoy making art again, and she invited Esther to help with her latest project, decorating the baby's room. Esther was thankful to be a part of this, and together they painted a beautiful image of the kingdom of Persia.

Esther also spent time getting to know Xerxes' five older children, visiting them in their separate quarters, along with Xerxes. He was such a loving father, and Esther thoroughly enjoyed seeing his face light up when he was with his sons and daughters.

Eventually, Vashti emerged from her room, softening, and calming down. Esther noticed she spoke in a caring manner with the other women. Once again, Esther gave thanks to God for being a miracle worker, this time in regard to Vashti. *God, I don't know why You saw fit to bring me to replace her, but I thank You we've both adjusted to our roles in the family and the kingdom. You are wonderful, God!*

Esther traveled with Xerxes quite a bit to various parts of the empire, both far and near from the palace. What a privilege and honor to accompany her husband, the king, to serve their people, together! Xerxes asked her what they could do to help people, especially women and children, be safer and healthier throughout Persia. It had really stuck with him how she said she hadn't felt safe in her life before she'd married him. To address this, they put together various programs to support the poor, children, orphans, widows, and women in general.

Particularly wonderful were their visits to Esther's own former neighborhood. She loved being in the company of Leenah, her former boss, showering her with gifts to support her bakery business, and paying visits to Uncle Mordecai. Over time, Esther noticed a change in her husband. She didn't see much of a difference between his public persona and his personal identity as Xerxes, the man. He was now one in the same. His countenance was more soft, less solemn, and people felt better approaching him, especially when Esther was around.

Uncle Mordecai and Leenah had bonded even more and had grown closer after Esther had gone to live in the palace. Esther was overjoyed when he shared the news with her that they had fallen in love and married! Her uncle had worked so hard for so many years to take care of her, and it truly made her happy to see him start his own family and life with Leenah. God was so good! It didn't surprise Esther at all. Her uncle and Leenah had clearly loved each other for so long, and in God's time, they had united as man and wife. God be praised!

Now that they were a family, Mordecai and Leenah would often come visit Esther at the palace, waiting outside the court of women. Hegai would open the door to them, and they would eat, talk, and visit together in the courtyard outside. What a blessing to have so many privileges as queen! Esther's heart felt so full, and she rejoiced in seeing her uncle's newlywed happiness! Mordecai was not old after all. In fact, he was six years younger than Esther's handsome husband!

Esther arranged for visits in the outer courtyard of the court of women for the other wives with their families too, plus for her maids and all the women who worked there to see their families. She loved using her queen privileges to bring happiness, not just for her, but for the other ladies living and working in the harem as well.

After she became queen, Xerxes had a new room made for her on the upper level of the harem with a balcony overlooking the courtyard. Delighted with this gift, she had given her old room downstairs to her seven maids. She didn't need that room anymore, and it would be nice for them to have their own space. Xerxes also gave Esther her own personal eunuch servant named Hathak. He came to be like a brother to Esther, like her maids had become like younger sisters. How nice to have siblings for the first time in her life! Indeed, she felt favored and blessed to have come to this royal family!

God, You never cease to amaze me!

When Leenah and Mordecai would visit, Leenah often brought pies and cakes from her bakery. Esther loved laughing with Leenah about how she had said she'd be making pies for a husband soon. Close enough! She brought the pies to Xerxes on the nights they were together, and he loved them just as much as she did. It felt so good to share her past with her husband, through pies of all things! If only she could tell him her whole story!

Perhaps the greatest miracle of all was when Vashti came to see Esther herself! One evening, as Esther was getting ready to meet Xerxes in the bridal chamber, there was a knock at her door.

"Esther? May I come in?"

"Yes, of course, Vashti."

Esther was a bit wary as Vashti hadn't spoken to her since she'd been chosen to be queen, but she had seen good changes in Vashti and was open to talk with her.

Esther opened the door, and Vashti came in. Gesturing toward the balcony table, Esther asked Vashti to sit down with her.

"Thanks for being okay to talk to me, Esther. I know I haven't been kind to you, and I'm sorry."

"Thank you, Vashti. I appreciate that."

"I'd like to explain myself if that's all right. I never should have been so mean to you, and I can't excuse that, but I want to share my story with you. I think it could be helpful for both of us."

"Sure. That sounds good. I'd like to hear it."

"I'll start at the beginning. I was brought to the harem when I was very young, a little younger than you. I wasn't afraid, but I also wasn't ready for what lay before me. Xerxes was the new king and had just started taking wives. He noticed I wasn't afraid of him, and he told me he liked that."

Esther nodded. He'd told her the same thing on their wedding night.

"It wasn't long before he told me he wanted to make me queen. That didn't scare me either. In fact, I was happy! I looked forward to the life of luxury and comfort."

"So what was the problem, Vashti? If you weren't scared and liked being queen, what went wrong?"

"That's just it, Esther. Nothing was wrong or would have been if I were someone else. But I'm not, I'm me. Hegai says some of the wives here are self-absorbed, and some are, but most aren't bad women, they're just simpler than you and me. We are the same in that way, Esther. You and I are more real than they are."

"How so?"

"I'm not putting down the other wives. Like I said, they're just more simple. They seem happy living this life with or without being in love with Xerxes. For you, I can tell it matters what you feel for him, and it did for me too. The difference is, you do feel for him, and I just didn't. It felt awful not loving the man I married and who clearly wanted us to be in love, even making me queen. Each time we slept together—"

Esther put up her hand. "It's okay, Vashti. You don't have to talk about that. It's so personal."

"Yes, it is, and I'm so sorry I asked you and in front of everyone about your wedding night! That was not okay. As for me, I'll just say

I started to hate myself more and more over time since I was just not able to love this man, and he wanted my love. He's a good man and he tried so hard, but I just didn't feel anything for him. I started to feel sick, physically sick inside. It wasn't healthy for me, and it wasn't fair to Xerxes. And when we slept together, I was always scared of getting pregnant since I didn't love him, and I felt that wouldn't be right.

"So you did get scared, eventually?"

"Yes. At first, I thought when he made me queen, that was a political move only, not a romantic gesture, but he's a romantic at heart. I hoped, as queen, I would only be a political figure, and he'd just move on to his other wives for his needs and his children. But no, he kept trying with me to get me to love him. So when he threw me that banquet, I knew it was my chance to put an end to the whole charade. I refused to show up, and that was the only way to make it clear to him that I don't want him."

"Did you know that would also mean giving up being queen?"

"He's a good man, and I knew he wouldn't hurt me. If giving up being queen was the price to pay, well, I wasn't happy with it, but I had to do what I had to do. I know I was bitter about not being queen anymore, and I took it out on you and the other wives, and I'm sorry. I also know I hurt Xerxes, and that means he was not in a good place when you married him and so that affects you in your marriage. I'm sorry about that too."

"Thanks for telling me your story, Vashti. It really means a lot. And life really isn't easy for anyone. I don't judge you. Like you said, you were so young when you came here, and it sounds like you just did the best you could each step of the way. Sometimes things just don't work out. And you're really sweet to apologize to me about it. Clearly, this wasn't an easy situation, and that's not your fault."

"You're so kind, Esther. Thanks."

"It's just the truth. Vashti, do you wish you could go back? Like, go back in time before you married Xerxes, or go back to where you lived before you came to the palace?"

"Not at all, I really feel like everything happens for a reason, and honestly, it just makes me so happy seeing you thrive as queen.

You're better at it than I was, and it really is for the best. Everyone can see that."

"Now you're being kind."

Vashti smiled. "As you said, it's just the truth."

"So you don't see yourself ever wanting to leave the palace and marry someone else?"

"No. I really am happy to stay here. Being part of this family has become meaningful for me. I think I've found my place, like the aunt figure for everyone, like how Hegai is the father of the wives and the other women who work here in the harem. Anyway, I don't really think marriage is for me."

"It's time for me to go meet Xerxes. Thanks so much for sharing with me, Vashti."

"Of course. Just one more thing. Xerxes never told me he loved me because he didn't, even though he wanted to and he tried so hard. But everyone knows he loves you, and I'm sure he will tell you soon if he hasn't already."

Esther hugged Vashti, she hugged her back, and they went their separate ways—Vashti, back downstairs to her room, and Esther to meet Xerxes in the bridal chamber.

That night, wrapped in each other's arms, Xerxes uttered the words Esther had been hoping for but also dreading: "Esther…I love you."

Tears welled up in her eyes, and she trembled. "You too," she whispered, kissing Xerxes's bare chest.

She couldn't bring herself to say the full sentence. Not when she hadn't shared her full heart with the man.

But it didn't matter anyway. By the sound of his rhythmic breathing, Esther knew her husband was already asleep.

CHAPTER 15

A Plot Discovered

Mordecai had never been more joyful! He was newlywed to Leenah, and both he and Esther were now happily married. From what he saw and heard of Xerxes, he seemed to be a good man. It seemed clear the man loved her, and she him. God had provided such a good life for them both! Who would have thought they'd both find love in a foreign land without their parents? God truly works wonders!

That night, the soldiers had abruptly arrived at the door and taken Esther away had been so frightening! He'd had a flashback to the soldiers on the doorstep who had killed their parents! Yet God had meant it for good, honoring their family by raising Esther up to be not only a wife of the king, but his queen wife! It was better than anything Mordecai could have ever hoped for!

His life with Leenah was much more comfortable than the life he'd lived while raising Esther. Thanks to Esther and Xerxes' generous help and gifts, both Leenah's bakery business and his butcher shop were doing so much better. He and Leenah were even able to renovate the house after she moved in. Best of all, in doing so, he was finally able to say goodbye to those hideous, blood-stained front steps. Thanks be to God! He'd never forget that day or the beloved memory of his and Esther's parents. Still, what a joy to not have that constant, sad reminder literally on his doorstep!

That also meant he no longer had to lie about the bloodstains since they were now gone. *Lord, forgive me for breaking your com-*

mandment to always tell the truth! You know I did so in order to keep Esther and I safe, and now I thank You for Your forgiveness and compassion, as well as no longer having to lie to protect us! Amen!

Most mornings, Mordecai would walk to the court of women to say hi to Esther. On this walk one day, as he was passing by the king's gate, he overheard a disturbing conversation. Two soldiers were apparently grumbling and complaining.

"I'm telling you, Bigthana! The king just isn't the same since he married that Esther. He's not tough like before. I bet he can't even protect us!"

"Well, what can we do about it, Teresh? The man is clearly in love, and why shouldn't he be? His wife is just gorgeous! I'd love to have her for myself, tell you the truth!"

The men snickered. Mordecai was repulsed! How dare they speak of his daughter that way!

"We are soldiers, and we are strong, even if our king has become weak. You asked, what can we do? Well, I'm not gonna just sit here and do nothing. Here's what we'll do. Let's take him out, and then have our fun with the little wifey, shall we?"

"Definitely! Tonight! But how?"

"Here's the plan! The king will most likely be in the bridal chamber with the queen. We'll pose as servants, bringing them refreshments, and when they open the door, we attack! First, we kill the king and then we enjoy his wife! Queen Esther of Persia indeed!"

They laughed and laughed. Mordecai was incredulous. How could these men be so deplorable and plan such a despicable plot! A moment ago, he'd been basking in the joy of his and Esther's new life, and now it had all come crashing down! God, are we returning to the days of Noah!

Well, he didn't need to hear any more from these men. Save Esther! Save the king!

Mordecai took off running. He had run to save Esther when she was a baby, and he would do the same now! He couldn't get to the court of women gate fast enough!

Lord, let me fly as if on eagles' wings! Please!

People stared at him as he ran down the street. He didn't care. As he arrived at the gate, he could only pray Esther would come outside soon.

Come on, Esther! Please, come soon!

He began to cry even as he attempted to calm himself. Even his old trick of focusing on the morning birds chirping wasn't working. It was as if he was running outside at night, crying, with baby Esther in his arms all over again! He was shaking, trembling, and sweating with fear and anxiety.

God, You are my only hope! Send Esther out now!

CHAPTER 16

Warning the Queen

Esther knew something was horribly wrong as soon as she saw Mordecai. He was shaking and crying. This looked a lot like when he would wake up from nightmares!

She ran to him, calling for Hegai to open the gate. He opened it and left her and Mordecai alone in the courtyard. Hegai was always very respectful that way.

Esther directed her uncle to a table in the shade, gave him a glass of water she'd brought from the kitchen, and sat down next to him. As he drank the water and breathed deeply, he did eventually calm down.

"Uncle, what is it? What's happened?"

"You're in danger, Esther, and Xerxes too! There's a plot for him to be killed, and they want to hurt you!"

Esther sighed. It always pained her to see Mordecai anxious and fretting.

"Uncle, I can see you're really upset, like you always were after nightmares. Are you sure you're not talking about one of those? Maybe you just dreamed about a plot? It is still morning after all, and you didn't wake up that long ago."

Mordecai looked at her then, shaking his head. "Daughter, please, I respect that you're not a little girl anymore. You're a grown woman with a husband. I love you and Xerxes, you are family. That's why I want to protect you two. Please, believe me and respect me that I know the difference between nightmares and reality. I know I have my issues, but I am not crazy."

Esther took his hands in hers.

"Uncle, you're right, and I'm sorry. Yes, I believe you. Tell me about this plot. How did you hear about it?"

"Like always, I was walking past the king's gate on my way here. I heard two men, the guards at the door, talking. Their names are Bigthana and Teresh."

Esther was shocked! Her uncle heard actual names! This must be real then! She was truly sorry she'd doubted him for a moment!

"Uncle, thanks so much for telling me! I will tell Xerxes tonight. He has already sent word for me to visit him then."

"That's too late. That will be too late, daughter! The men are planning to kill him right there in the bridal chamber tonight! You have to tell Xerxes right this minute!"

"Oh, wow! Okay, Uncle, I think I can manage that. Xerxes should be in the throne room right now, and you know it's against the law for anyone to approach him while he's in there due to the sensitive nature of his political meetings. But since he already sent for me to visit him tonight, I think it will be okay."

"He loves you, Esther. Of course, it will be okay! Now go, daughter, go!"

Esther kissed her uncle's hands and hurried out of the courtyard, heading toward the harem exit and then on to the throne room.

As she ran, Esther thought back to what Hegai had told her the day after her wedding. True love means making sacrifices, even facing danger, for the other person. In this case, she was taking a risk by breaking the law in entering the throne room when she hadn't been called there. But she knew this risk was worth it because she was doing so to protect both her and Xerxes. He loved her and wouldn't let anything happen to her, even if she had to break the law to deliver this news. She trusted him, and above all, she had courageous faith and trust in God. She prayed the same short prayer she had on her wedding night.

God, be with me.

CHAPTER 17

God Save the King

At the door of the throne room, Esther said another brief prayer, this time, for her husband.

God, please protect Xerxes. Please don't let me be too late!

She opened the door and saw him in the distance on his throne. He smiled at her. Encouraged, she made her way down the aisle. He held out the golden scepter to her, a sign that she was permitted to speak.

She breathed a sigh of relief! Now no one could protest to her arrival, as the king himself had shown his approval.

"My king, may you live forever!"

"Thank you, my queen. What brings you to the throne room?"

"My uncle Mordecai has just been the bearer of dreadful news! He has just told me he overheard on his way over to see me today, a plot for your life and to take me by force as well!"

Xerxes's face fell.

"Who! Who would dare plot such a thing! Who is he, and where is he!"

"My uncle has two names. Bigthana and Teresh. They said they are planning this very night to do this crime!"

"Guards! Haman and Suleman! Bring to me Bigthana and Teresh! Now!"

The men guarding Xerxes on his throne went out quickly to bring in the men in question.

The throne room was a very solemn place. Xerxes and Esther both knew not to drop their formal royal roles even when left alone in there together. Still, their eyes on each other said it all. The emotions of fear at the situation and love for each other filled the room.

After a few agonizing moments, the throne room guards returned, dragging Bigthana and Teresh behind them.

Haman and Suleman threw them at the king's feet. At this point, only he could determine their fate.

"What do you have to say for yourselves!" Xerxes demanded. "I have it on good authority you two were plotting against myself and the queen! You have ten seconds to tell me your side of the story! Go!"

"I was just going along with it to test Bigthana, Your Majesty! It's a long time since I suspected he was up to something!"

"No, it was all you! All you, Teresh!"

"I've heard enough! Guards, take them outside and hang them up on a tree! You will not hurt me or the queen. Let justice be done to put evil away from the kingdom!"

As the guards dragged them back outside, Xerxes followed, taking Esther by the hand. They walked outside together to see the end of these men's lives. As they passed through the king's gate together, Esther saw Mordecai at the side, also keeping watch. She beckoned to him, and he followed behind.

They approached a tree in the middle of the square at the front of the palace. A large crowd had gathered and was cheering.

"Let justice be done! Put evil away from the kingdom!" yelled Xerxes.

With that, the two men were killed.

Esther, Mordecai, and Xerxes all breathed a collective sigh of relief.

Esther hugged her uncle, crying.

"Thank you so much, Mordecai!" Xerxes put his arms around both Esther and Mordecai.

Esther met Xerxes' eyes. The look on his face made it clear he really needed to take comfort with her that night. She felt the same way, of course.

Xerxes had done his part to protect her, so had Mordecai. But above all, God had come through, as always.

Thank You, God, for saving both myself and my beloved husband, the king. Amen!

CHAPTER 18

Mordecai Reveals His Faith

The next morning, Xerxes woke up, ready to face the day. Esther was still asleep, so he simply kissed her forehead and rose from the bed. After bathing and dressing, he headed straight to the throne room. A promotion was in order today, for the man who had dragged the traitors outside yesterday, Haman.

Sitting on the throne, Xerxes spoke to the guard on his left side.

"Haman, thank you for your help yesterday. You really stepped up in my moment of need to protect both me and the queen. You clearly took the lead in the execution of the traitors and getting rid of them as soon as possible. I'd like to promote you to my second-in-command. How's that?"

Haman bowed before him.

"I only did my duty to you and the queen, Your Majesty! Thank you so much, and I appreciate your recognition!"

Xerxes nodded.

"Of course. I will walk you outside to the king's gate and publicly announce your new position. After the announcement, feel free to take the rest of the day off. You earned it yesterday. Follow me."

The two men walked together outside to the gate. Xerxes raised his voice and spoke to the people.

"All should bow down and do reverence to Haman, my new second-in-command! Yesterday, he came through to bring the traitors to justice and protect myself and the queen! Respect and bow to him when you see him in my gate!"

The people clapped as Xerxes nodded and walked back inside to the throne room.

Mordecai was standing close by, approaching the gate on his way to the court of women to see Esther.

God, I know I cannot bow down to a man. I only serve You!

All the others were bowing down before Haman. He noticed and walked up to Mordecai, furious.

"Did you or did you not hear the king, Mordecai! Who do you think you are! What, do you think the rules don't apply to you! Do you not fear your king! Bow down to me now! I am the king's second-in-command! Bow down now! Now!"

God, I will not deny You. I will not deny You! I have kept my faith hidden all my life for fear, but now I can't hide who I am or deny You! I won't do it, Lord!

Mordecai swallowed and prepared himself to speak the truth in public for the first time.

"Sir, I respect you are the king's choice for second-in-command, and I congratulate you on that. But I cannot bow down to anyone but God. Because I am a Jew."

Saying it out loud for everyone to hear was like breaking an evil curse. Suddenly, Mordecai didn't feel afraid of anything anymore. Praise Yahweh!

Haman was having none of it.

"If you don't bow down to me, I promise you will be sorry, you dirty Jew!"

He sneered and walked away, heading toward his house.

CHAPTER 19

Plot against the Jews

Haman entered his home and slammed the door behind him loudly.

"What's that all about!" His wife, Zeresh, was not amused.

When he didn't answer right away, she followed with more impatient questions.

"So? How'd it go then? Did you get that promotion or not? We have debts to pay, man! I hope you got some recognition today!"

Haman sat down at the kitchen table, defeated. "Yes, I did get it."

Zeresh sat down.

"Then why does your face look how it does? What's wrong? We've been waiting and hoping for this position for so long, and now when it comes, you look like you'd rather be dead! Speak up, man! What's going on!"

Haman sighed. "As soon as I got the promotion, Xerxes walked me outside to the king's gate and asked all to bow down and reverence me when I pass by."

"Sounds good to me so far."

"Will you let me finish?"

"Finish then!"

"One man wouldn't bow down to me, Mordecai. He's the queen's uncle. I always knew there was something different about him, but today, he revealed what he is: a filthy Jew!"

Zeresh pounded her hand on the table angrily.

"Those Jews! They should have all gone back many years ago when Cyrus sent that decree! Why did they stay!"

"Your guess is as good as mine. They are crazy, all of them. Always talking about their god. Ha! Well, he said he can't bow down to a man, only to God. Where is this God of the Jews anyway? We can't see Him at all."

"Exactly. He doesn't exist. It's just a figment of their imagination as an excuse to cause trouble. Listen, don't let him get you down forever, husband. Now that you got this promotion, use it for good. Stamp out any rebellion or sign of disrespect! Convince the king to wipe out the Jews from the empire!"

Haman sat back in the chair and took a long exhale.

"Sure, that sounds great, but how do you propose I do that?"

Zeresh stood up and poked Haman's head.

"You have a big head, you just need to learn how to use it, my husband. You're close to the king now, second-in-command. Tell him there is a group of people who have it out against the laws of Persia who won't obey. Mordecai wouldn't obey the order to do reverence to you, and he's a Jew, so it's just a tiny stretch of the truth, is it not?"

Haman's eyes widened, following her logic. "You're right, you're right! That's what I'll do. Today, the king gave me the day off. Let's take the time to strategize a plan! We need to figure out exactly what I'll say to the king."

"Just a word of caution, my husband. Maybe, don't tell the king you are speaking of the Jews. That Mordecai is a strange one and so is his niece, the queen. They're both Jews, which of course makes so much sense now. The king is clearly in love with the queen, so he won't agree to the order if you say the people in question are the Jews."

He frowned, concerned.

"Really? Leave out such a crucial piece of information as that? Trick the king?"

Zeresh threw her hands up, exasperated. Then she sat down again by his side.

"Do I have to do everything around here! Look, it's the only way to get what we want, so yes, this is what must be done! And you know what? Shame on that Mordecai for not reverencing my husband. We should prepare something really special for him, a special way out, a torturous death. Not just torturous but humiliating too! He should be hung in the public square just like those two traitors! Tomorrow, see to it that you have a hanging post set up, fifty feet high. That's where he can meet his end!"

Haman grinned, looking at his wife. "How did I ever get so lucky as to have such a conniving woman?"

"Stick with me, and you'll go far. Now, come on, we have busy days ahead of us to strategize all these things."

They planned far into the night, a plot against the Jews, which made them cackle with joy.

CHAPTER 20

Mordecai and Leenah at Home

After a long day's work, Mordecai returned home. Leenah opened the door for him, gave him a quick hug and a kiss, and then saw the dejected look on his face.

"What is it? What's wrong?"

Mordecai sat down at the table.

"I'll tell you, but first, let me hear how your day was. That's how Esther and I always started our evenings when she got back from work."

Leenah smiled and sat down next to him.

"I know, and you've been such a good father to her all these years. But she's a married woman now, and so am I. I'm your wife. You can share everything with me. I'm fine, really, thanks for asking, got a lot of business today at the bakery, but I can tell you're not okay. What is it, my love?"

He sighed. Leenah. He'd loved her since he was a young boy even though he didn't yet know what love was at that time. His and Esther's parents had always kept them in the house to keep them safe, but somehow, fate had connected them when he glimpsed Leenah walking by the house one afternoon, and they started talking, striking up their friendship, which had blossomed into love over time. And he loved her even more now. She'd been patient all those years with waiting for him to be ready, and now that she was here, she was just so wonderful.

Finally, Mordecai felt more or less safe in life, with Leenah as his true helpmate, to walk by his side. Even though it went against the rules he'd indoctrinated into Esther, he couldn't hold back and told Leenah on their wedding night that he was a Jew. To his delight, she said she also believed in his God! She'd come to believe it since Jews had survived so much over so many centuries, it just made logical sense. She confided she'd come to faith in her late teens, and this had helped comfort her a great deal when she'd lost both her parents to an illness. How wonderful to not have to hide who he was anymore, especially from his dear wife. He looked at her now, ready to tell her of the day's events.

"Remember my latest scare? That was when I overheard yesterday the plot to kill the king and rape Esther. The traitors were put to death, hung in the square in front of the palace. One of the men who dragged them out is named Haman. Today, the king brought him out to the gate, presented him as second-in-command, and said we have to bow down to him and do reverence. You know I'm fine with respect, and I respect and even love the king—he's Esther's husband. But something about that Haman doesn't sit well with me. He seems fake, hypocritical, selfish. At any rate, we only bow down to God. So he got upset. I explained that I cannot bow down to a man because I am a Jew."

Leenah gasped. "You've never publicly revealed that, Mordecai! How did you feel about that? Are you afraid? Talk to me, I'm here for you!"

He grinned. "That's just it, I don't feel scared, Leenah! For the first time in my life! It felt so good to just say it right there! Just like breaking an evil spell. The truth is out there, and it's okay! I lived in fear all these years from when I was a boy and Esther's and my parents were murdered, but that was a long time ago. It seems times have changed. Xerxes wasn't even the king at that time. The king we have now is kind and respects our family, more than that he's married to Esther and clearly loves her."

Leenah threw her arms around Mordecai in a warm embrace.

"I'm so glad you are doing so much better, Mordecai! That's amazing! And yes, I see no reason to fear either. Praise God!"

She wiped away happy tears from her eyes.

"Okay, so then, why did you look sad when you came in here? I don't understand that part."

"It just made me disappointed, his reaction to it. He called me a dirty Jew and then walked away."

She shook her head.

"Well, consider the source. He's not a very classy individual, right? So why should we care what he thinks?"

Mordecai laughed. She always was able to find the humor in any situation.

"Right, right. I know you're right, Leenah. I just hate to think he carries that attitude about his own queen. Esther's a Jew of course."

"Did you talk to her about this today?"

"No, I didn't want to worry her. I think we're still not completely over what happened yesterday."

Leenah nodded.

"Well, not to worry. I'm sure it'll all be fine. Esther is queen, and you said so yourself that the king loves her. No harm should come her way. And as for you, you're clearly feeling a lot better and safer. Now that I've seen you're in a much better place, I can tell you some happy news! I've actually been getting a lot of customers at the shop lately who are talking openly about being Jewish. They're not scared anymore! We have so many brothers and sisters in faith all around us and didn't even know it! Praise Yahweh!"

Mordecai was stunned but happy with this surprising news.

"So all these years I was in hiding and didn't need to be? All this time… God, thank You so much for protecting us either way and providing us with a family of faith! I need to meet these people, Leenah!"

"Of course! I'll introduce you. There are so many of them!"

They talked long into the night as they enjoyed the latest treats from Leenah's bakery shop.

CHAPTER 21

Tricking the King

A few weeks later, after perfecting his plan with Zeresh, Haman got up early at the crack of dawn. He wanted to be first to enter the throne room, waiting for the king to the left of the throne. When Xerxes approached, he nodded his head in reverence.

Haman wasted no time whatsoever, speaking up as soon as Xerxes sat on his throne.

"May I speak, Your Majesty?"

Xerxes smiled. "Sounds like you already are, Haman. What is it?"

"Your Majesty, some disturbing news has come to my attention. There is a people scattered throughout the kingdom who keep themselves separate. They have different customs, and they don't respect your laws! It's clearly not in your best interest to put up with this people. Therefore, if I may so humbly suggest, you should make a decree to destroy them."

A frown slowly formed on Xerxes's face.

"These sound like some pretty sweeping generalizations, very sensational as well. Who are these people? And wouldn't I know about something like this? Where are you getting your information from, Haman?"

Haman drew a quick, nervous breath.

"Do you have any reason to doubt me, Your Majesty? After the other day, you know I only have your best interest at heart."

Xerxes nodded with a touch of distrust.

"Right. It would seem that way. I just wonder why you're hesitant to say who these people are. Shouldn't I know?"

"I don't know their name, just that they refuse to obey orders and they are strange—"

A dismissive wave of Xerxes's hand said it all, making Haman be quiet again.

"All right, Haman, if this is really true, then yes, something should be done about it before it gets out of hand. It seems these people haven't been identified by name yet. Let's not let it get to that point then, right? Listen, take my ring and make the order, signing it with my hand thereby. As soon as you're done, come back here. We have many other important things to discuss today in the throne room with other nobles and politicians. Don't waste too much time on something that should be easy to take care of."

With that, Xerxes handed over his king's signet ring. Haman gratefully grabbed it, hastily bowed, and ran from the room, so happy he almost dropped it!

Xerxes watched him disappear, shaking his head and wondering why Haman was acting so strangely that morning. *But no matter*, he thought to himself, *there are a million other things on my list for today*. In fact, it was the most busy time of the year in politics. New nobles coming to visit almost every day! This was the time of year Xerxes dreaded. Today was also the first anniversary of when Vashti had rejected him with all those painful memories of hurt and humiliation. He took a deep breath, sighed, and then changed his thoughts to Esther, smiling. His beautiful queen bride, and the love of his life. What a good thing he had found in her! Such a generous and kind woman, and the perfect one for him. He knew she loved him, although she only showed him instead of telling him for some reason.

He'd told her of his love for her a few months into the marriage before drifting off to sleep one night, but Esther had yet to say it. It didn't really bother him since she showed him love, and so abundantly! Indeed, it did his heart good to see her as much as possible, and that's why he'd decided as soon as they met he would send for her every other night. But this was a different season, and he'd been so busy this time of year once again; it had been a few weeks without a visit from his beloved Esther. It pained him to go so long without seeing her, and he missed her more than he felt he could bear. He'd explained to her beforehand how the busy political time was approaching, and he'd be using the four weeks ahead, not only to work hard on political strategies but also to tend to his other wives' needs, sending for another one each night. They, of course, needed attention too. By this time, it had been almost a month without seeing Esther, and he planned to see her in just a few more days. He'd assured her he wouldn't let a month go by without sending for her again. *Okay, get to work Xerxes, come on, focus*, he told himself. The visiting nobles then arrived, and the day flew by after that, thankfully.

CHAPTER 22

What's the Matter with Mordecai?

Esther looked out across her balcony. She was sitting at the table outside, taking in the peace of the early morning. She never took it for granted, the sense of peace she had found in her new life here with Xerxes in the palace. Sipping her morning tea Hathak had brought to her, she prayed to God in her heart as usual.

God, thank You for all my creature comforts in the palace, the family I've found here and the love of my wonderful husband, the king. Thank You that Mordecai and Leenah have also found love, that Mordecai has become healthier with less fear since marrying Leenah, and that together we put a stop to an evil plan. Lord, You know the thoughts and intents of my heart. You know what I want most is to share my full heart with Xerxes, the way I do with You. But I am still hesitating. Please, God, give me a sign that it is time. Amen.

Even as she prayed, Esther knew something else was bothering her. It had been almost a month since she'd seen her Xerxes. She missed him so much her heart ached. He had been considerate to explain to her in advance this was the busiest political season when he had so much work and wanted to use it for that and to give attention to the other wives, one by one each night. She understood those points, but it hurt her to know how well she knew his heart while he did not know hers. It had been almost a year to the day she had entered the palace after Vashti had disrespected the king. Esther knew Xerxes was being reminded of all the shame and disillusionment of that event and was filling his time by diving into work during the day and fulfilling his marriage duties for his other wives one by one each night. He was a strong and noble man, and she saw right through him. She'd seen it in his face on their wedding night when she asked him about Vashti. He still wasn't over the pain. If only he would allow himself to be vulnerable in her arms, she would be there for him.

But how can I really be there for him if I haven't shared my origins with him yet? Esther sighed, dismissing the thought.

Hathak approached and sat down beside her. "How are you, my lady? Missing your man, I see."

Esther nodded, wiping away a tear. "I know, I'm so obvious! He is burying himself in work and other family duties. He doesn't want to be with me right now since he doesn't want to fall apart, remembering Vashti's rejection."

"Love seems a hard thing to navigate, my queen. I'm sorry for the pain."

"You're such a good friend, just like a brother to me, Hathak. Loving someone is indeed painful sometimes, but Hegai explained to me the day after my wedding that love requires sacrifice. That means considering what the other person needs. The thing is, in this case, I'm what he needs, he just isn't ready to face all the emotions. But I will be patient. Love is patient. He told me he wouldn't let a month pass without sending for me, so only a few days left."

"You are very kind and very strong. That's why he chose you, Esther."

"Thanks, Hathak. You are so good to me, as always. Thanks for this tea! Is it a new one?"

"Yes, I put cinnamon in it today. Glad you like it!"

Esther looked away into the distance, her thoughts turning to Mordecai. Suddenly, as if in direct answer to her thoughts, he appeared! To her surprise, he was wearing sackcloth and ashes, the apparel of one who is in mourning!

Hathak noticed her face changed and followed her gaze.

"Esther, is that your uncle down there? Why is he dressed like that?"

"I don't know, Hathak, but this deeply troubles me. Please, go outside and ask him what's going on. He won't come into the women's courtyard dressed like that. He's sending me some type of message. Go, quickly!"

Hathak left, and Esther kept her eyes fixed on her uncle. Just a few moments later, she saw Hathak approach to talk to him. The conversation indeed seemed frantic. *God, what could this be about?* Hathak left Mordecai and Esther waited for him, with baited breath, praying, *Lord, whatever is happening, give me wisdom and strength to face it. Please, don't let it be the worst...*

When Hathak returned to the room, Esther could hold back no longer.

"Is Leenah dead?"

Her voice was squeaking with emotion. Seeing her uncle by himself, in mourning apparel, and without his wife by his side had sent her into panic mode, assuming Leenah had been killed like her parents and grandparents all those years ago!

"No, my lady, no one is dead, but Mordecai fears your people will die soon! He has overheard a plot being spoken of by the king's gate, a plot to kill the Jews. Esther, I didn't know you are a Jewess?"

She nodded, proudly.

"Yes, I am a Jew, just like my uncle, but he always raised me to hide my origins, so I would be safe. Our parents were killed for being Jews."

Hathak gasped. "I'm so sorry, my queen! Does the king know?"

She sighed. Now was the time indeed to tell Xerxes. She was relieved yet anxious.

"No, I haven't told him. At first, it was out of fear, but then when I met him on our wedding night, he was so kind to me. I've been keeping it a secret ever since because it's the path of least resistance. But I do long to share my true identity with him. Now is the time! Tell me of this plot."

"Mordecai overheard a decree has been written with the king's ring by that Haman, the new second-in-command, to kill all the Jews, young and old, women and children! This would be a massacre throughout the empire! Esther, you have to stop this! Mordecai said if you don't speak up, God can deliver your people by some other way. Yet it seems you have become queen for this very reason, for such a time as this."

She nodded, following. Indeed, Esther had prayed the day she became queen to use her power for good. She had always tried to do that, but now was the most obvious time, to save her people!

"Thanks so much for delivering me the message, Hathak! We all know it is against the law for anyone to enter the throne room, unless the king has called for them. As I said, Xerxes hasn't called for me for almost a month at this point, but I can't wait any longer! I must tell him of this, and I know how I will do it. First, I will tell him who I am and then reveal this plot. God made me queen for a reason, and I have to fight for my people. If not, how can I even call myself a queen! I will do what is right! I know Xerxes loves me and won't want to kill me for entering the throne room without permission beforehand, but if someone else says otherwise and if I have to die, so be it. Here's what I'll do, tell this to Mordecai. Tell him to gather up all the Jews in the region and fast, not drinking or eating for three days. Hathak, you and I and my maids will do the same. At the end of the three days, I will go to the king. If I die, at least I will die doing something for my people."

Hathak nodded and turned around, quickly, delivering this message to Mordecai. Esther saw her uncle look up at her with a look of pride. This was her time to speak up for her people, and she could tell Mordecai was no longer afraid. Neither was she.

CHAPTER 23

Queen before the King

Bright and early on the third day, Esther rose, bathed, and dressed, and put on her royal garments. Today was the first anniversary of her wedding night with Xerxes. Now, it was time to go to him again, but she would tell him who she really was. She had no fear, only faith. Perfect love casts out fear after all, and that's what she felt for this man. *God, be with me as You were with me that day and always, the first day I met my husband. Let me speak well and continue to win his favor. Grant me wisdom to show him who I am, and that my people cannot be erased from the world. Amen!*

She walked to the throne room, standing outside. Xerxes sat on his throne, surrounded by his guards, nobles, and visiting politicians. He noticed her standing outside and smiled. Just as she expected, he held out the golden scepter to her, and she approached. She walked halfway to his throne and then bowed her head.

"If it pleases the king, I would like to be alone in here with you without the guards, nobles, and politicians, just you and me."

When she lifted her head up again, she saw Xerxes nodding. Then he opened up his mouth to speak. "You heard the queen. Everyone, please give us some time together. I will let you know when you can return to the throne room."

The guards, nobles, and politicians looked confused, but of course obeyed without question. The king had spoken! Quickly and quietly, they shuffled their way outside and closed the door to the throne room behind them.

As soon as they were gone, Xerxes leaned forward on his throne. "Esther, please come to me. Now."

She could hear the longing in his voice and how much he had missed her. Esther ran to him then as if she were a little girl! He picked her up and sat her on his lap, and they exchanged a tender embrace, lasting for several minutes. It was so good to be with him again!

Xerxes spoke first. "Esther, I've missed you so much. I'm so glad to see you! I was going to send for you tonight since I can't go another day without you. I'm so sorry for taking so long. Listen, I was thinking about it the other day, and I know what was holding me back from you these days. One year ago was our wedding when we met, and I just didn't want to face all those feelings of how I felt at that time. When we met, I thought I was a failure as a king and as a man, rejected by my queen wife at the time. But I see that wasn't the right way to respond to this, instead I should have reached out to you, my true queen. I'm so sorry, and it also wasn't fair to you. Can you forgive me, Esther?"

She buried her head in his chest, crying softly. Then she raised her head up once more.

"Of course, I forgive you, Xerxes. I don't hold this against you at all, and I know your heart, so I didn't take it personally. I just tried to be patient, but today I couldn't wait any longer to see you. I tried to be as patient as I could, but this was the end of my rope, and I just had to come here. Is that okay? I know it is against the law since you hadn't called for me yet."

Xerxes grinned. "It should be obvious that it's okay, Esther. Aren't you sitting here on my lap right now? Of course, it's okay. You really should be able to come to the throne room anytime. You should always be in here with me. In fact, I was just thinking today I will have another throne made for you so you can always be by my side in here. You're my queen, and I trusted you since we met, so you should be in here with me at all times. It was ridiculous to not have a throne set up for you since day one."

Esther laughed and played with his hair. "But, Xerxes, I like sitting on your lap!" she teased.

He gave her a sideways look. "Esther. You know how much I like it too, but that's not the point!" He laughed.

How good it was to hear the sound of his laugh! One of her favorite sounds in the world!

"Besides wanting to see me, what did you need to talk about? You know I will give you anything you want, even half the kingdom!"

"I know, and I thank you for being so generous and kind with me as always. What I want is the same thing you want. I will wait for you at the bridal chamber tonight so we can be together. I will have a private banquet prepared for us there. There's something I want to share with you tonight. And tomorrow, let's have a banquet in the public dining hall of the palace, which I will also have prepared for us."

His eyes lit up with emotion, and he bit his lip. Esther knew he was trying not to cry, understanding the significance of her gesture. Vashti hadn't come to the banquet he'd made for her, but Esther was preparing a banquet for him.

"You…you would really do that, Esther?" His voice was heavy with emotion.

She smiled and kissed his cheek. "Of course."

"That is so kind. Thank you. And it will be so good for us to have more time together, especially after so long. I will see you tonight at the bridal chamber. I'll be there as soon as I can. Please, on your way out, tell the men they can return."

She nodded and walked out of the throne room. *Thank You, God! All is indeed going well! I knew it would!*

CHAPTER 24

Esther Gives Her Whole Heart

Esther returned to her room, rejoicing.

"Hathak, please go downstairs and tell my maids all is going according to plan! I will see Xerxes tonight and tell him who I am. Then I'll reveal the plot at tomorrow night's banquet. And I know you all are as hungry as I am from fasting, so now it's time to eat!"

"I'll tell them right away and then cook us up a meal in the kitchen!"

Hathak turned to deliver the joyous news to the maids.

After eating with Hathak and her maids, Esther spent the day in prayer.

At nightfall, Esther made her way to the bridal chamber. Shortly after her arrival, Xerxes opened the door.

He went to her, put his arms around her, then stood back, taking her hands in his. "Is it what I'm thinking, Esther? Are we having a child, my love?"

"Oh…no, Xerxes, that's not what I want to tell you. That's not my news. I can see how happy that would have made you, and I'm sorry to disappoint, but no, I'm not pregnant."

"Don't apologize. It's okay! You are very young, and it can take a little while. And as for disappointing me, you never do that, always the opposite, in fact! I admire you so much, Esther. You know that. What is it you wanted to tell me then?"

Esther drew a deep breath, ready to speak the truth.

"Remember when I asked you how you feel about Jews on our wedding night? I was actually asking you how you feel about my people."

Xerxes looked surprised but not upset.

"Your people, the Jews. You are a Jewess then, Esther? I just don't understand why you thought you couldn't say so. We've been married for a year now. Were you afraid to tell me?"

"Forgive me, Xerxes. I know how much you wanted us to be close since you explained your search for your true queen on our wedding night. Please, understand this wasn't about you and I never wanted to hide my true self in our marriage. I actually grew up dreaming about having complete openness with my husband, if I ever married. But I was raised a different way. My uncle Mordecai always wanted me to be safe, and since our parents were killed for being Jews when I was only three, he raised me to never tell anyone, even a husband, about my origins. I'm so sorry, Xerxes."

"I am so sorry too for what you've been through, Esther! And it goes even deeper than that, right? I know Hebrews have had a difficult history. Pharaoh was cowardly enough to have your babies put to death, out of fear of rebellion. I guess your people have lived in fear of extermination for so long, it's just always there on some level. I think I understand that, and no, this isn't something I hold against you."

"Thanks so much for understanding!"

"Of course! Esther, I meant everything I said on our wedding night. That goes for whether you're Jewish or not, and whether I knew or not. You are my wife, and I take care of my own. You're also my queen wife, and I knew you were the right one since we met. And above all that, Esther, I am deeply in love with you. You are always safe with me. I would never let anything happen to you, ever. If need be, I would fight to protect you with my bare hands! You have not only the heart of a queen. You have the heart of a mother for the people. I see how wonderful you are with my children as well. Thank you for being you and for telling me more about who you are. Now I can understand you better. I love you so much!"

Xerxes drew her to him and leaned down to kiss her.

Esther pulled away, playfully. "Xerxes, are you saying you're trying to get me pregnant with those comments about me as a mother?"

"Well, technically, I'm always trying to get all my wives pregnant. I'm a king and need many heirs. But yes, to answer your question, I would love to have a child with you, if God grants it."

He ran his fingers through her hair and cupped her face in his hands.

"And let me be very clear about this. When I say God, I am speaking about your God. The God of Abraham, Isaac, and Jacob."

"Xerxes… I love you!" She was finally able to say it. Esther leapt into his arms, kissing him.

As they made love, Esther fully surrendered her heart to Xerxes.

CHAPTER 25

Mordecai Is Honored by the King

Xerxes woke up in the middle of the night. Esther was sound asleep. He kissed her forehead and got up from the bed. He just couldn't sleep. Things kept going around and around in his head. He put on a robe and headed to the king's meeting room. Sometimes, going over old documents helped him soothe his anxiety and get back to sleep.

So much had happened today! It was like a whirlwind! Esther had come to him, forgiven him of his stupidity at pushing her away this past month, and they'd had a sweet reunion. Esther had also said some new things to him that night, revealing she was a Jewess and also telling him she loved him for the first time. In fact, perhaps that was why she was able to tell him finally since she'd told him about her origins. Xerxes was ashamed of himself for not making her feel safe enough to tell him about her beliefs. She always wanted to feel safe and said she felt that way with him since their wedding night. But clearly not enough to break her old habits of staying in the shadows regarding her faith. Why couldn't he be a better husband? Why hadn't he been able to make her feel completely safe, or at least enough to tell him who she was?

As he pondered all this, he came across a paper that summarized the events of when Mordecai had discovered Bigthana and Teresh's plot on his life and to hurt the queen. Had nothing been done to honor and reward Mordecai? How could he have overlooked this? He'd honored Haman for dragging the traitors to the trees to be killed, but he'd forgotten to recognize Mordecai! *Better late than never. I will raise up Mordecai tomorrow, first thing.* With that, he went back to sleep beside his beloved Esther.

In the morning, Xerxes headed straight for the throne room. Haman was there, waiting for him as usual.

After sitting on his throne, Xerxes wasted no time. "Haman, what should be done for the man who the king delights to honor?"

Haman's eyes brightened, and it was clear he thought the king was speaking of him.

Not so, thought Xerxes, *not this time.*

"I would say, bring a royal robe of the king's for him, along with the king's horse, plus, give him a royal crest. Then, have one of the king's nobles ride with him throughout the streets, proclaiming, 'This is a man the king delights to honor!'"

"Excellent. Haman, please go get Mordecai the Jew outside the king's gate and do everything you have said. Spare no detail you have mentioned. Go!"

Frowning, Haman slowly turned around and reluctantly did all that was asked of him. Mordecai the Jew was to be honored while he was humiliated to do this for the man who wouldn't bow down to him. He couldn't believe how cruel and unjust this was!

Meanwhile, Esther was watching everything from the window of the bridal chamber. She saw Mordecai being escorted through the city in a royal robe and crest. How nice that Xerxes had honored her uncle! What a kind and fitting gesture. She was grinning from ear to ear for pride. *Thank You, God. Indeed, You have lifted up the lowly, first me, and now my uncle. God be praised!*

Esther also had to appreciate God's sense of humor. Haman had an evil thought against Mordecai and the Jews and had turned it into a plan to annihilate them all. Instead, God had now orchestrated Haman's humiliation as Xerxes had ordered him to parade Mordecai around the city with royal flair! It was the exact opposite of what Haman had wanted for Mordecai!

Lord, You are so funny, and You really know how to make a point! Thank You for comforting me with not only the love of my husband who now knows my true heart, but also this sight in front of me! My uncle is being honored by my husband, and I know that means You will save us through Xerxes! Please give my beloved man the strength and courage to bear the shock of my announcement tonight at the banquet. I know it will be difficult for him, and I just hope he is not too hard on himself. This was not his fault, and anyway, You will help him make it right. Amen.

As the hours went by, she made herself ready for the banquet. Then, it was time.

CHAPTER 26

The Banquet

Esther hurried into the banquet hall, excited to make sure everything was set up just right. Sure enough, the food was ready and displayed lavishly. Nobles and politicians were arriving to the banquet, as well as the guards, including Haman, the enemy. *Good*, Esther thought. He needed to be here as well, so she could reveal the man for who he really was to her husband.

She took her place at the head of the table, and when Xerxes entered the hall, everyone stood up. When he took his place next to Esther, everyone sat down and began feasting and chatting.

As they ate, Xerxes leaned into Esther. "What do you want most, Esther? You know I would give you anything, even half the kingdom as I told you before."

"Xerxes, you know I don't need anything. I have everything I need, and more. But since you asked, there is something more I must tell you."

She raised her voice so the entire room would hear. This was the time to speak loudly, to expose the evil plot in the sight and ears of everyone there.

"If it pleases the king, let my life and the life of my people be given to me. Let us be saved! For we have been sold, my people and I, to be killed!"

The room became silent at this horrifying announcement. Xerxes's face showed his anger, and Haman at his side began to tremble and crouch down in fear.

Xerxes stood up, his countenance like fire. "Who is this man, and where is he! Who would dare to do such a thing!"

Esther pointed her finger at Haman. "It is this wicked Haman who is both our adversary and enemy!"

Xerxes was so upset he got up from the table and left, walking outside to the palace garden, pacing angrily back and forth. When he couldn't take it anymore, he fell to his knees. He began to pray, out loud, with tears streaming down his face.

"God! The God of Abraham, Isaac, and Jacob! The God of my queen bride, Esther! I know I've never spoken to You, and I never truly believed until Esther told me she is a Jew, but I know You can hear me! I know You are a just and compassionate God, freeing Your people from slavery all those years ago and taking care of them so they can be part of my kingdom today, even bringing Esther to me as queen! God, thank You so much for her, she is such a gift! You know I've always tried my best, but I keep making mistakes. I can't do this without You, God. I chose the wrong queen the first time, then I didn't know there was a plot for my life and against Esther, then I forgot to honor Mordecai for delivering the message. I was stupid and pushed my queen away when I needed her most! I even hurt her in the process! I hurt the one woman I truly love! I wasn't able to make her feel safe enough to tell me of her belief in You! And now this! This is the worst thing imaginable! The man I thought was my friend, who is eating at the table next to my Esther, wants to kill her and her people, Your people! God, I can't handle this. I can't fix all my mistakes. I'm not strong enough on my own! Please, God, I need You! I know You have spoken to Your people in the past, and I don't know if You will speak to me now, but please give me a sign so I can know what to do! I am weak, but You are strong! Help me, God!"

Slowly, Xerxes stood up, looking up at the night sky and wiping away his tears. He turned around and headed inside.

Back in the banquet hall, Haman lunged at Esther, grabbing her clothes.

"Why did you do this! Now he will kill me!"

At that moment, Xerxes returned, aghast at what he saw. Was this man touching his beloved Esther! He ran at him, grabbed him by the throat, and pulled Haman off of Esther.

"Don't you ever come near my queen! How dare you!" He flung Haman to the ground.

At that moment, a servant approached Xerxes, gently placing a hand on his shoulder.

"Yes, Harbona, what is it?"

"Your Majesty, if I may, look outside at that hanging post fifty feet high this Haman has constructed. What do you think we should do with him?"

Without hesitation, Xerxes yelled, "Hang him on it! Get him out of here, now!"

The guards took Haman away, kicking and screaming.

Xerxes sat down, breathing deeply. When he was somewhat calm, he put his face in his hands.

"Esther, I feel like such a fool! This man was someone I thought cared about us! I even recently promoted him! How could this happen! I promise you, I didn't know this was a scheme to kill you and your people! He said they were an unidentified group, not Jews! I gave him my signet ring, and he made and signed the order, but I promise you I didn't know!"

"I know, Xerxes! I believe you! You're not a fool, Xerxes. He was indeed evil, a trickster and a liar! It's not about you. He was a bad man. He was jealous and covetous. Sometimes, bad people are jealous of good people. He was also envious of my uncle, which is how this all started. This is not your fault, what Haman did. God let it happen this way so you could save me and my people. You are my strong, sweet Xerxes, and I love you so much! Now more than ever! My love, you're a hero."

Xerxes found the courage to look at her and then gave a small, defeated laugh.

"I hardly feel like a hero right now, Esther! You're being so kind and generous as always. I said I would always protect you, and thankfully, I wasn't too late. Thanks be to God! I'll issue an order to reverse the plot Haman concocted. Your parents were right to name you after a myrtle tree. You have enriched and have grown my heart, our family, and our kingdom, as a myrtle tree reaches up to God in heaven. You are a hero too, my love. Now come with me."

Xerxes took Esther's hand in his. They walked together to the balcony and looked over their kingdom God had given them. The enemy was now dead. They would be able to rest, live, work, love, and worship God, now, in peace. Amen and amen!

EPILOGUE

True to King Xerxes' order, Jews throughout the kingdom were able to legally defend themselves if attacked. Mordecai joined together with many others to turn his butcher shop into a station for making armor and all types of weapons. Farmers brought Mordecai their plowshares and pruning hooks to be made into swords. Indeed, it was a day spoken by the prophets when pruning hooks were turned into spears (Joel 3:10).

At the end of this, there was peace throughout the kingdom, and many were so impressed by the might of the Jews that they also became believers in the God of Abraham, Isaac, and Jacob. King Xerxes brought Mordecai and Leenah to live in the palace, and Mordecai was promoted to second-in-command, next to the king himself.

Esther's family was now complete, happy, and joyful, all together in the palace. She indeed found true love as she'd always wished for as a young girl, seeing God raise her up in the kingdom to save her people, and witness her faith to all Persia. The Persian Empire was made both magnificent and peaceful especially after Esther became queen. Yet like all empires, it later fell. Now Esther, Xerxes, Mordecai, Leenah, Hegai, Hathak, and Vashti all wait in the dust for the day of resurrection. On that day, the Messiah, Jesus Christ, will return to bring the one Kingdom that will never end, the Kingdom of God on Earth. May God bless everyone who reads this book and make them part of that Kingdom to come. Amen!

"The seventh angel sounded his trumpet, and there were loud voices in heaven which said, 'The Kingdom of the world has become the Kingdom of the Lord and of his Christ, and he shall reign forever and ever!'" (Rev. 11:15).

BIBLE ACCOUNT OF ESTHER

Chapter 1

This is what happened during the time of Xerxes, the Xerxes who ruled over 127 provinces stretching from India to Cush. At that time, King Xerxes reigned from his royal throne in the citadel of Susa, and in the third year of his reign, he gave a banquet for all his nobles and officials. The military leaders of Persia and Media, the princes, and the nobles of the provinces were present.

For a full 180 days, he displayed the vast wealth of his kingdom and the splendor and glory of His Majesty. When these days were over, the king gave a banquet, lasting seven days, in the enclosed garden of the king's palace, for all the people from the least to the greatest who were in the citadel of Susa. The garden had hangings of white and blue linen, fastened with cords of white linen and purple material to silver rings on marble pillars. There were couches of gold and silver on a mosaic pavement of porphyry, marble, mother-of-pearl, and other costly stones. Wine was served in goblets of gold, each one different from the other, and the royal wine was abundant, in keeping with the king's liberality. By the king's command, each guest was allowed to drink with no restrictions, for the king instructed all the wine stewards to serve each man what he wished.

Queen Vashti also gave a banquet for the women in the royal palace of King Xerxes.

On the seventh day, when King Xerxes was in high spirits from wine, he commanded the seven eunuchs who served him—Mehuman, Biztha, Harbona, Bigtha, Abagtha, Zethar, and Karkas—to bring before him Queen Vashti, wearing her royal crown, in order to display her beauty to the people and nobles, for she was lovely to look at. But when the attendants delivered the king's command, Queen Vashti refused to come. Then the king became furious and burned with anger.

Since it was customary for the king to consult experts in matters of law and justice, he spoke with the wise men who understood the times and were closest to the king—Karshena, Shethar, Admatha, Tarshish, Meres, Marsena, and Memukan, the seven nobles of Persia and Media who had special access to the king and were highest in the kingdom.

"According to law, what must be done to Queen Vashti?" he asked. "She has not obeyed the command of King Xerxes that the eunuchs have taken to her."

Then Memukan replied in the presence of the king and the nobles, "Queen Vashti has done wrong, not only against the king but also against all the nobles and the peoples of all the provinces of King Xerxes. For the queen's conduct will become known to all the women, and so they will despise their husbands and say, 'King Xerxes commanded Queen Vashti to be brought before him, but she would not come.' This very day the Persian and Median women of the nobility who have heard about the queen's conduct will respond to all the king's nobles in the same way. There will be no end of disrespect and discord."

"Therefore, if it pleases the king, let him issue a royal decree, and let it be written in the laws of Persia and Media, which cannot be repealed, that Vashti is never again to enter the presence of King Xerxes. Also let the king give her royal position to someone else who's better than she. Then when the king's edict is proclaimed throughout all this vast realm, all the women will respect their husbands, from the least to the greatest."

The king and his nobles were pleased with this advice, so the king did as Memukan proposed. He sent dispatches to all parts of the kingdom, to each province in its own script and to each people in their own language, proclaiming that every man should be ruler over his own household, using his native tongue.

Chapter 2

Later, when King Xerxes' fury had subsided, he remembered Vashti and what she had done and what he had decreed about her. Then the king's personal attendants proposed, 'Let a search be made for beautiful young virgins for the king. Let the king appoint commissioners in every province of his realm to bring all these beautiful young women into the harem at the citadel of Susa. Let them be placed under the care of Hegai, the king's eunuch, who is in charge of the women, and let beauty treatments be given to them. Then let the young woman who pleases the king be queen instead of Vashti." This advice appealed to the king, and he followed it.

Now there was in the citadel of Susa a Jew of the tribe of Benjamin, named Mordecai son of Jair, the son of Shimei, the son of Kish, who had been carried into exile from Jerusalem by Nebuchadnezzar, king of Babylon, among those taken captive with Jehoiachin, king of Judah. Mordecai had a cousin named Hadassah, whom he had brought up because she had neither father nor mother. This young woman, who was also known as Esther, had a lovely figure and was beautiful. Mordecai had taken her as his own daughter when her father and mother died.

When the king's order and edict had been proclaimed, many young women were brought to the citadel of Susa and put under the care of Hegai. Esther also was taken to the king's palace and entrusted to Hegai, who had charge of the harem. She pleased him and won his favor. Immediately, he provided her with her beauty treatments and special food. He assigned to her seven female attendants selected from the king's palace and moved her and her attendants into the best place in the harem.

Esther had not revealed her nationality and family background because Mordecai had forbidden her to do so. Every day he walked back and forth near the courtyard of the harem to find out how Esther was and what was happening to her.

Before a young woman's turn came to go in to King Xerxes, she had to complete twelve months of beauty treatments prescribed for the women, six months with oil of myrrh, and six with perfumes and cosmetics. And this is how she would go to the king: Anything she wanted was given her to take with her from the harem to the king's palace. In the evening, she would go there and in the morning return to another part of the harem to the care of Shaashgaz, the king's eunuch who was in charge of the concubines. She would not return to the king unless he was delighted with her and summoned her by name.

When the turn came for Esther (the young woman Mordecai had adopted, the daughter of his uncle Abihail) to go to the king, she asked for nothing other than what Hegai, the king's eunuch who was in charge of the harem, suggested. And Esther won the favor of everyone who saw her. She was taken to King Xerxes in the royal residence in the tenth month, the month of Tebeth, in the seventh year of his reign.

Now the king was attracted to Esther more than to any of the other women, and she won his favor and approval more than any of the other virgins. So he set a royal crown on her head and made her queen instead of Vashti. And the king gave a great banquet, Esther's banquet, for all his nobles and officials. He proclaimed a holiday throughout the provinces and distributed gifts with royal liberality.

When the virgins were assembled a second time, Mordecai was sitting at the king's gate. But Esther had kept secret her family background and nationality just as Mordecai had told her to do, for she continued to follow Mordecai's instructions as she had done when he was bringing her up.

During the time Mordecai was sitting at the king's gate, Bigthana and Teresh, two of the king's officers who guarded the doorway, became angry and conspired to assassinate King Xerxes. But Mordecai found out about the plot and told Queen Esther, who in turn reported it to the king, giving credit to Mordecai. And when the report was investigated and found to be true, the two officials were impaled on poles. All this was recorded in the book of the annals in the presence of the king.

Chapter 3

After these events, King Xerxes honored Haman, son of Hammedatha, the Agagite, elevating him and giving him a seat of honor higher than that of all the other nobles. All the royal officials at the king's gate knelt down and paid honor to Haman, for the king had commanded this concerning him. But Mordecai would not kneel down or pay him honor.

Then the royal officials at the king's gate asked Mordecai, "Why do you disobey the king's command?" Day after day, they spoke to him, but he refused to comply. Therefore, they told Haman about it to see whether Mordecai's behavior would be tolerated, for he had told them he was a Jew.

When Haman saw that Mordecai would not kneel down or pay him honor, he was enraged. Yet having learned who Mordecai's people were, he scorned the idea of killing only Mordecai. Instead, Haman looked for a way to destroy all Mordecai's people, the Jews, throughout the whole kingdom of Xerxes.

In the twelfth year of King Xerxes, in the first month, the month of Nisan, the *pur* (that is, the lot) was cast in the presence of Haman to select a day and month. And the lot fell on the twelfth month the month of Adar.

Then Haman said to King Xerxes, "There is a certain people dispersed among the peoples in all the provinces of your kingdom who keep themselves separate. Their customs are different from those of all other people, and they do not obey the king's laws. It is not in the king's best interest to tolerate them. If it pleases the king, let a decree be issued to destroy them, and I will give ten thousand talents of silver to the king's administrators for the royal treasury."

So the king took his signet ring from his finger and gave it to Haman, son of Hammedatha, the Agagite, the enemy of the Jews. "Keep the money," the king said to Haman, "and do with the people as you please."

Then on the thirteenth day of the first month, the royal secretaries were summoned. They wrote out in the script of each province and in the language of each people all Haman's orders to the king's satraps, the governors of the various provinces and the nobles of the various peoples. These were written in the name of King Xerxes himself and sealed with his own ring. Dispatches were sent by couriers to all the king's provinces with the order to destroy, kill, and annihilate all the Jews—young and old, women and children—on a single day, the thirteenth day of the twelfth month, the month of Adar, and to plunder their goods. A copy of the text of the edict was to be issued as law in every province and made known to the people of every nationality so they would be ready for that day.

The couriers went out, spurred on by the king's command, and the edict was issued in the citadel of Susa. The king and Haman sat down to drink, but the city of Susa was bewildered.

Chapter 4

When Mordecai learned of all that had been done, he tore his clothes and put on sackcloth and ashes and went out into the city, wailing loudly and bitterly. But he went only as far as the king's gate because no one clothed in sackcloth was allowed to enter it. In every province to which the edict and order of the king came, there was great mourning among the Jews, with fasting, weeping, and wailing. Many lay in sackcloth and ashes.

When Esther's eunuchs and female attendants came and told her about Mordecai, she was in great distress. She sent clothes for him to put on instead of his sackcloth, but he would not accept them. Then Esther summoned Hathak, one of the king's eunuchs assigned to attend her, and ordered him to find out what was troubling Mordecai and why.

So Hathak went out to Mordecai in the open square of the city in front of the king's gate. Mordecai told him everything that had happened to him, including the exact amount of money Haman had promised to pay into the royal treasury for the destruction of the Jews. He also gave him a copy of the text of the edict for their annihilation, which had been published in Susa, to show to Esther and explain it to her, and he told him to instruct her to go into the king's presence to beg for mercy and plead with him for her people.

Hathak went back and reported to Esther what Mordecai had said. Then she instructed him to say to Mordecai, "All the king's officials and the people of the royal provinces know that for any man or woman who approaches the king in the inner court without being summoned the king has but one law: that they be put to death unless the king extends the gold scepter to them and spares their lives. But thirty days have passed since I was called to go to the king."

When Esther's words were reported to Mordecai, he sent back this answer: "Do not think that because you are in the king's house, you alone of all the Jews will escape. For if you remain silent at this time, relief and deliverance for the Jews will arise from another place, but you and your father's family will perish. You came to the Kingdom for such a time as this."

Then Esther sent this reply to Mordecai: "Go, gather together all the Jews who are in Susa and fast for me. Do not eat or drink for three days, night or day. I and my attendants will fast as you do. When this is done, I will go to the king, even though it is against the law. And if I perish, I perish."

So Mordecai went away and carried out all of Esther's instructions.

Chapter 5

On the third day, Esther put on her royal robes and stood in the inner court of the palace, in front of the king's hall. The king was sitting on his royal throne in the hall, facing the entrance. When he saw Queen Esther standing in the court, he was pleased with her and held out to her the gold scepter that was in his hand. So Esther approached and touched the tip of the scepter.

Then the king asked, "What is it, Queen Esther? What is your request? Even up to half the kingdom, it will be given you."

"If it pleases the king," replied Esther, "let the king, together with Haman, come today to a banquet I have prepared for him."

"Bring Haman at once," the king said, "so that we may do what Esther asks."

So the king and Haman went to the banquet Esther had prepared. As they were drinking wine, the king again asked Esther, "Now what is your petition? It will be given you. And what is your request? Even up to half the kingdom, it will be granted."

Esther replied, "My petition and my request is this: If the king regards me with favor and if it pleases the king to grant my petition and fulfill my request, let the king and Haman come tomorrow to the banquet I will prepare for them. Then I will answer the king's question."

Haman went out that day happy and in high spirits. But when he saw Mordecai at the king's gate and observed that he neither rose nor showed fear in his presence, he was filled with rage against Mordecai. Nevertheless, Haman restrained himself and went home.

Calling together his friends and Zeresh, his wife, Haman boasted to them about his vast wealth, his many sons, and all the ways the king had honored him and how he had elevated him above the other nobles and officials. "And that's not all," Haman added. "I'm the only person Queen Esther invited to accompany the king to the banquet she gave. And she has invited me along with the king tomorrow. But all this gives me no satisfaction as long as I see that Jew Mordecai sitting at the king's gate."

His wife Zeresh and all his friends said to him, "Have a pole set up, reaching to a height of fifty cubits, and ask the king in the morning to have Mordecai impaled on it. Then go with the king to the banquet and enjoy yourself." This suggestion delighted Haman, and he had the pole set up.

Chapter 6

That night, the king could not sleep; so he ordered the book of the chronicles, the record of his reign, to be brought in and read to him. It was found recorded there that Mordecai had exposed Bigthana and Teresh, two of the king's officers who guarded the doorway who had conspired to assassinate King Xerxes.

"What honor and recognition has Mordecai received for this?" the king asked.

"Nothing has been done for him," his attendants answered.

The king said, "Who is in the court?" Now Haman had just entered the outer court of the palace to speak to the king about impaling Mordecai on the pole he had set up for him.

His attendants answered, "Haman is standing in the court."

"Bring him in," the king ordered.

When Haman entered, the king asked him, "What should be done for the man the king delights to honor?"

Now Haman thought to himself, *Who is there that the king would rather honor than me?* So he answered the king, "For the man the king delights to honor, have them bring a royal robe the king has worn and a horse the king has ridden, one with a royal crest placed on its head. Then let the robe and horse be entrusted to one of the king's most noble princes. Let them robe the man the king delights to honor and lead him on the horse through the city streets, proclaiming before him, 'This is what is done for the man the king delights to honor!'"

"Go at once," the king commanded Haman. "Get the robe and the horse and do just as you have suggested for Mordecai the Jew, who sits at the king's gate. Do not neglect anything you have recommended."

So Haman got the robe and the horse. He robed Mordecai and led him on horseback through the city streets, proclaiming before him, "This is what is done for the man the king delights to honor!"

Afterward, Mordecai returned to the king's gate, but Haman rushed home, with his head covered in grief, and told Zeresh his wife and all his friends everything that had happened to him.

His advisers and his wife Zeresh said to him, "Since Mordecai, before whom your down fall has started, is of Jewish origin, you cannot stand against him—you will surely come to ruin!" While they were still talking with him, the king's eunuchs arrived and hurried Haman away to the banquet Esther had prepared.

Chapter 7

So the king and Haman went to Queen Esther's banquet, and as they were drinking wine on the second day, the king again asked, "Queen Esther, what is your petition? It will be given you. What is your request? Even up to half the kingdom, it will be granted."

Then, Queen Esther answered, "If I have found favor with you, Your Majesty, and if it pleases you, grant me my life—this is my petition. And spare my people—this is my request. For I and my people have been sold to be destroyed, killed, and annihilated. If we had merely been sold as male and female slaves, I would have kept quiet because no such distress would justify disturbing the king."

King Xerxes asked Queen Esther, "Who is he? Where is he— the man who has dared to do such a thing?"

Esther said, "An adversary and enemy! This vile Haman!"

Then Haman was terrified before the king and queen. The king got up in a rage, left his wine, and went out into the palace garden. But Haman, realizing that the king had already decided his fate, stayed behind to beg Queen Esther for his life.

Just as the king returned from the palace garden to the banquet hall, Haman was falling on the couch where Esther was reclining.

The king exclaimed, "Will he even molest the queen while she is with me in the house?"

As soon as the word left the king's mouth, they covered Haman's face. Then Harbona, one of the eunuchs attending the king, said, "A pole reaching to a height of fifty cubits stands by Haman's house. He had set it up for Mordecai, who spoke up to help the king."

The king said, "Impale him on it!" So they impaled Haman on the pole he had set up for Mordecai. Then the king's fury subsided.

Chapter 8

That same day, King Xerxes gave Queen Esther the estate of Haman, the enemy of the Jews. And Mordecai came into the presence of the king, for Esther had told how he was related to her. The king took off his signet ring, which he had reclaimed from Haman, and presented it to Mordecai. And Esther appointed him over Haman's estate. Esther again pleaded with the king, falling at his feet and weeping. She begged him to put an end to the evil plan of Haman the Agagite, which he had devised against the Jews. Then the king extended the gold scepter to Esther, and she arose and stood before him.

"If it pleases the king," she said, "and if he regards me with favor and thinks it the right thing to do, and if he is pleased with me, let an order be written overruling the dispatches that Haman, son of Hammedatha, the Agagite, devised and wrote to destroy the Jews in all the king's provinces. For how can I bear to see disaster fall on my people? How can I bear to see the destruction of my family?"

King Xerxes replied to Queen Esther and to Mordecai the Jew, "Because Haman attacked the Jews, I have given his estate to Esther, and they have impaled him on the pole he set up. Now write another decree in the king's name in behalf of the Jews as seems best to you and seal it with the king's signet ring—for no document written in the king's name and sealed with his ring can be revoked."

At once, the royal secretaries were summoned—on the twenty-third day of the third month, the month of Sivan. They wrote out all Mordecai's orders to the Jews, and to the satraps, governors, and nobles of the 127 provinces stretching from India to Cush. These orders were written in the script of each province and the language of each people and also to the Jews in their own script and language. Mordecai wrote in the name of King Xerxes, sealed the dispatches with the king's signet ring, and sent them by mounted couriers, who rode fast horses especially bred for the king.

The king's edict granted the Jews in every city the right to assemble and protect themselves; to destroy, kill, and annihilate the armed men of any nationality or province who might attack them and their women and children, and to plunder the property of their enemies. The day appointed for the Jews to do this in all the provinces of King Xerxes was the thirteenth day of the twelfth month, the month of Adar. A copy of the text of the edict was to be issued as law in every province and made known to the people of every nationality so that the Jews would be ready on that day to avenge themselves on their enemies.

The couriers, riding the royal horses, went out, spurred on by the king's command, and the edict was issued in the citadel of Susa.

When Mordecai left the king's presence, he was wearing royal garments of blue and white, a large crown of gold and a purple robe of fine linen. And the city of Susa held a joyous celebration. For the Jews, it was a time of happiness and joy, gladness, and honor. In every province and in every city to which the edict of the king came, there was joy and gladness among the Jews, with feasting and celebrating. And many people of other nationalities became Jews because fear of the Jews had seized them.

Chapter 9

On the thirteenth day of the twelfth month, the month of Adar, the edict commanded by the king was to be carried out. On this day, the enemies of the Jews had hoped to overpower them, but now the tables were turned, and the Jews got the upper hand over those who hated them. The Jews assembled in their cities in all the provinces of King Xerxes to attack those determined to destroy them. No one could stand against them because the people of all the other nationalities were afraid of them. And all the nobles of the provinces, the satraps, the governors, and the king's administrators helped the Jews because fear of Mordecai had seized them. Mordecai was prominent in the palace; his reputation spread throughout the provinces, and he became more and more powerful.

The Jews struck down all their enemies with the sword, killing and destroying them, and they did what they pleased to those who hated them. In the citadel of Susa, the Jews killed and destroyed five hundred men. They also killed Parshandatha, Dalphon, Aspatha, Poratha, Adalia, Aridatha, Parmashta, Arisai, Aridai, and Vaizatha, the ten sons of Haman, son of Hammedatha, the enemy of the Jews. But they did not lay their hands on the plunder.

The number of those killed in the citadel of Susa was reported to the king that same day. The king said to Queen Esther, "The

Jews have killed and destroyed five hundred men and the ten sons of Haman in the citadel of Susa. What have they done in the rest of the king's provinces? Now what is your petition? It will be granted."

"If it pleases the king," Esther answered, "give the Jews in Susa permission to carry out this day's edict tomorrow also, and let Haman's ten sons be impaled on poles."

So the king commanded that this be done. And edict was issued in Susa, and they impaled the ten sons of Haman. The Jews in Susa came together on the fourteenth day of the month of Adar, and they put to death in Susa three hundred men, but they did not lay their hands on the plunder.

Meanwhile, the remainder of the Jews who were in the king's provinces also assembled to protect themselves and get relief from their enemies. They killed seventy-five thousand of them but did not lay their hands on the plunder. This happened on the thirteenth day of the month of Adar, and on the fourteenth, they rested and made it a day of feasting and joy.

The Jews in Susa, however, had assembled on the thirteenth and fourteenth, and then on the fifteenth, they rested and made it a day of feasting and joy.

That is why rural Jews—those living in villages—observe the fourteenth of the month of Adar as a day of joy and feasting, a day for giving presents to each other.

Mordecai recorded these events, and he sent letters to all the Jews throughout the provinces of King Xerxes, near and far, to have them celebrate annually the fourteenth and fifteenth days of the month of Adar as the time when the Jews got relief from their enemies, and as the month when their sorrow was turned into joy and their mourning into a day of celebration. He wrote them to observe the days as days of feasting and joy and giving presents of food to one another and gifts to the poor.

So the Jews agreed to continue the celebration they had begun, doing what Mordecai had written to them. For Haman, son of Hammedatha, the Agagite, the enemy of all the Jews, had plotted against the Jews to destroy them and had cast the *pur* (that is, the lot) for their ruin and destruction. But when the plot came to the king's attention, he issued written orders that the evil scheme Haman had devised against the Jews should come back onto his own head, and that he and his sons should be impaled on poles. (Therefore, these days were called Purim, from the word *pur.*) Because of everything written in this letter and because of what they had seen and what had happened to them, the Jews took it on themselves to establish the custom that they and their descendants and all who join them should without fail observe these two days every year, in the way prescribed and at the time appointed. These days should be remembered and observed in every generation by every family, and in every province and in every city. And these days of Purim should never fail to be celebrated by the Jews—nor should the memory of these days die out among their descendants.

So Queen Esther, daughter of Abihail, along with Mordecai the Jew, wrote with full authority to confirm this second letter concerning Purim. And Mordecai sent letters to all the Jews in the 127 provinces of Xerxes' kingdom—words of goodwill and assurance—to establish these days of Purim at their designated times, as Mordecai the Jew and Queen Esther had decreed for them, and as they had established for themselves and their descendants in regard to their times of fasting and lamentation. Esther's decree confirmed these regulations about Purim, and it was written down in the records.

Chapter 10

King Xerxes imposed tribute throughout the empire to its distant shores. And all his acts of power and might, together with a full account of the greatness of Mordecai, whom the king had promoted, are they not written in the book of the annals of the kings of Media and Persia? Mordecai the Jew was second in rank to King Xerxes, preeminent among the Jews, and held in high esteem by his many fellow Jews because he worked for the good of his people and spoke up for the welfare of all the Jews.

BIBLE REFERENCES BY CHAPTER

Chapter 1: A Myrtle Tree Grows in Persia

Title inspired by the novel *A Tree Grows in Brooklyn* by Betty Smith.

1. "The same nightmare, right?" Esther wondered why she even asked. It had been the same since she was a little girl, too young to remember the murder of her parents along with Mordecai's.

   Mordecai looked at his niece, the only person left in their family. He had been young when their parents were killed, and she was only three at the time. Sixteen years later, and nightmares were still a recurring event in their home. Mordecai could only thank God Esther had been too young to recall what he'd witnessed on that horrendous day.

   Now there was in the citadel of Susa a Jew of the tribe of Benjamin, named Mordecai the son of Jair, the son of Shimei, the son of Kish, who had been carried into exile from Jerusalem by Nebuchadnezzar King of Babylon, among those taken captive with Jehoiachin King of Judah. Mordecai had a cousin named Hadassah, whom he had brought up because she had neither father nor mother. (Esther 2:5–7)

Chapter 2: All in a Day's Work

1. "God, Your word is a lamp to my feet and a light to my path." Direct quote from Psalm 119:105.
2. God knew her heart.

    For the word of God is living and active, sharper than any two-edged sword, piercing to the division of soul and spirit, of joints and of marrow, and discerning the thoughts and intentions of the heart. (Heb. 4:12).

3. Now she was a woman, and so beautiful.

    This young woman, who was also known as Esther, had a lovely figure and was beautiful. (Esther 2:7)

Chapter 3: Big News

1. "When I try to think about what I would want in marriage, I imagine being able to tell my husband everything in my heart and mind, like I do with God."

    Humble yourselves therefore under the mighty hand of God, that He may exalt you in due time: casting all your care upon Him; for He cares for you. (1 Pet. 5:7)

2. "Why can't it be? Why can't we return to a simpler time, like how Adam and Eve were in the Garden together with God?"

    He created them male and female, and He blessed them and named them Man in the day when they were created. (Gen. 5:2)

3. "What happened next, Esther! Within just a few generations, Adam and Eve's children were raping and killing each other! That's why God sent the Flood to put an end to that!"

So, God said to Noah, "I am going to put an end to all people, for the earth is filled with violence because of them. I am surely going to destroy both them and the earth." (Gen. 6:1)

4. King Xerxes has become displeased with Queen Vashti and has put her away. He now seeks a new queen for his kingdom. All young virgins are being summoned to the harem, and he will choose the most beautiful to be his queen.

Later when King Xerxes' fury had subsided, he remembered Vashti and what she had done and what he had decreed about her. Then the King's personal attendants proposed, "Let a search be made for beautiful young virgins for the King. Let the King appoint commissioners in every province of his realm to bring all these beautiful young women into the harem at the citadel of Susa. Let them be placed under the care of Hegai, the King's eunuch, who is in charge of the women; and let beauty treatments be given to them. Then let the young woman who pleases the King be Queen instead of Vashti." This advice appealed to the King and he followed it. (Esther 2:1–4)

5. "Go with these men, and I will be outside the court of the women every day to check on you. Being the wife of a king is a great honor. Maybe this is for the best or even what God has planned for you! And even if not, remember, God

is always with us, a sure help in times of trouble. Now go! Don't make the men wait! I love you, daughter!"

Every day he walked back and forth near the courtyard of the harem to find out how Esther was and what was happening to her. (Esther 2:11)

God is our refuge and strength, always ready
to help in times of trouble. (Ps. 46:1)

Chapter 4: Entering the Harem

1. "Welcome, lady. I am Hegai, head eunuch and keeper of the women. Follow me."

    It was if she could hear Mordecai's voice in her head. *Obey, daughter, obey!*

    When the King's order and edict had been proclaimed, many young women were brought to the citadel of Susa and put under the care of Hegai. Esther also was taken to the King's Palace and entrusted to Hegai, who had charge of the harem. (Esther 2:8)

    And whether you turn to the right or to the
    left, your ears will hear a voice behind you saying,
    "This is the way; walk in it." (Isa. 30:21)

2. "Listen up, girl, since you'll find I don't like to repeat myself. To your right is the kitchen. You girls will be getting special meals for your figure to be perfect. To the left is the beauty salon where you'll be getting all the fancy treatments: nails, hair, makeup, waxing, perfume, everything. You want to look your best when you go see the king. Down the hall to the right is your sleeping quarters. By quick assessment of looking at you, you won't need many treatments. You're

already pretty and have a great figure. In fact, I'd say you can go to the king tomorrow for your turn. Any questions?"

Before a young woman's turn came to go in to King Xerxes, she had to complete twelve months of beauty treatments, prescribed for the women, six months with oils of myrrh, and six with perfumes and cosmetics. (Esther 2:12)

3. "Listen girl, I need to put on a tough face since most girls here need it to whip them into shape. But you're different, I can tell. You actually care about Vashti, asked about her, the poor dear. Plus, you're smart. Instead of being self-absorbed like many girls here, you're looking ahead to the future and starting to do your research so you can truly please the king. Well done! I'm impressed. Tell you what. I'll take you to Vashti, and then I'll take you to a private room for yourself. You don't have to sleep in the common quarters with the others. I like you. You've won my favor. Now, follow me. I'll take you to Vashti's room."

She pleased him and won his favor. Immediately he provided her with beauty treatments and special food. He assigned to her seven female attendants selected from the King's Palace and moved her and her attendants into the best place in the harem. (Esther 2:9)

4. "Lord, it sounds like Vashti disrespected the king and he has put her away from him, like King David did with his first wife Michal since she despised him in her heart, making sure she was taken care of, but not going to her ever again."

As the ark of Yahweh was entering the city of David, Michal, daughter of Saul watched from a window. And when she saw King David dancing and leaping before Yahweh, she despised him in her heart. (2 Sam. 6:16)

And Michal daughter of Saul had no children to the day of her death. (2 Sam. 6:23)

Chapter 5: Making Herself Ready

Title referenced in Revelation 19:7, a bride who makes herself ready.

1. Hegai was there with seven girls.
   "Good evening, Esther. These are your seven maidens I've provided you. They can help you with whatever you need."
   Esther was shocked. What more could she want or need, never mind seven maids to help her with it!

   He assigned to her seven female attendants selected from the King's Palace and moved her and her attendants into the best place in the harem. (Esther 2:9)

Chapter 6: Father of the Bride

Title inspired by the film *Father of the Bride,* starring Steve Martin and Diane Keaton.

1. Esther walked in, and Hegai closed the door behind her, making Esther think of when God shut the door of Noah's ark. Would she be safe in here as God had protected Noah and his family?

   She was taken to King Xerxes in the royal residence in the tenth month, the month of

Tebeth, in the seventh year of his reign. (Esther 2:16)

The animals going in were male and female, of every living thing, as God had commanded Noah. Then Yahweh shut him in. (Gen. 7:16)

Chapter 7: One Night with the King

Title inspired by the film *One Night with the King*, film directed by Michael O. Sajbel.

1. Esther was caught off guard. What a thing to ask! Such a personal question!

    For the word of God is alive and active. Sharper than any double-edged sword, it penetrates even to dividing soul and spirit, joints and marrow; it judges the thoughts and attitudes of the heart. (Heb. 4:12)

2. As soon as you came into this palace, you legally became my wife. I'm a man who takes care of his own. You are part of this family and will be taken care of here, forever. That goes for any child you give me too.

    For the unbelieving husband has been sanctified through his wife, and the unbelieving wife has been sanctified through her believing husband. Otherwise, your children would be unclean, but as it is, they are holy. (1 Cor. 7:14)

3. "Right. Thank you. I can see you are a very good man."

    God saw all that he had made, and it was very good. (Gen. 1:31)

4. "My grandfather, King Cyrus, freed the Hebrew captives and let them go back to Israel."

In the first year of Cyrus king of Persia, in order to fulfill the word of the LORD spoken by Jeremiah, the LORD moved the heart of Cyrus King of Persia to make a proclamation throughout his realm and also to put it in writing: "This is what Cyrus King of Persia says: 'The LORD, the God of heaven, has given me all the kingdoms of the earth and he has appointed me to build a temple for him at Jerusalem in Judah. Any of his people among you may go up to Jerusalem in Judah and build the temple of the LORD, the God of Israel, the God who is in Jerusalem, and may their God be with them. And in any locality where survivors may now be living, the people are to provide them with silver and gold, with goods and livestock, and with freewill offerings for the temple of God in Jerusalem." (Ezra 1:1–4)

Chapter 8: Decision Day

Title inspired by Lifetime channel reality TV series, *Married at First Sight*.

1. He was so attractive, in both face and physique! Eyes and skin like dark chocolate, with muscle definition throughout his whole body!

His eyes are as the eyes of doves by the rivers of waters, washed with milk and fitly set: his cheeks are as a bed of spices as sweet flowers: his lips like lilies dropping sweet smelling myrrh: his hands are as gold rings set with the beryl: his belly is as bright ivory overlaid with sapphires: his legs are as pillars of marble, set upon sockets of fine gold: his countenance is as Lebanon, excellent as the cedars. (Song of Solomon 5:12–15)

2. *God, I know Uncle Mordecai was right. We can't go back to the Garden time of Adam and Eve. But now, I know You made it to be such a nice experience, man and wife coming together as one flesh. Thank You, God, for this gift!*

For this reason, a man shall leave his father and mother and be joined to his wife; and they will become one flesh. (Gen. 2:24)

3. Esther smiled. It sounded a lot like what God promised for when the Messiah would come. Security and peace for all. *Thank You, God, for this blessing! Maybe I really am safe with this man?*

In his days Judah will be saved and Israel will live in safety. This is the name by which he will be called: Yahweh our righteous savior. (Jer. 23:6)

This is what Yahweh says: "I will return to Zion and dwell in Jerusalem. Then Jerusalem will be called the faithful city, and the mountain of Yahweh almighty will be called the holy mountain. This is what Yahweh almighty says, 'Once again men and women of ripe old age will sit in the streets of Jerusalem, each of them with cane in hand because of their age. The city streets will be filled with boys and girls playing there.'" (Zech. 8:3–5)

4. 4. Esther felt for him. Suddenly, she longed to hug him but felt that would be inappropriate. It was one thing to

embrace the man last night while he was taking her as his wife. It was another to do so in the light of day, entirely on her own. She stayed still.

> A time to embrace and a time to refrain
> from embracing. (Eccles. 3:5)

Chapter 9: Xerxes Reflects and Shares the News

1. She carried herself with royalty yet humility. What a queen he had found!

   > But you are a chosen people, a royal priest-
   > hood, a holy nation, God's special possession,
   > that you may declare the praises of Him who
   > called you out of darkness into His wonderful
   > light. (1 Pet. 2:9)

2. As he had explained to Esther, his wives seemed afraid or distant toward him. This was especially true on the wedding night, when it was a wife's first time. No matter how caring and gentle he tried to be, no wife had ever truly engaged with him. It seemed clear to Xerxes that a man should not feel alone while in the conjugal act. Yet as ironic and pathetic as it was, that was exactly how he had always felt, alone in his marriage bed. It had always been the same, every time, with every wife, ever since Xerxes' own first time with the first wife he'd taken. But not so last night with Esther! No, not at all!

   > Jerusalem, Jerusalem, you who kill the
   > prophets and stone those sent to you, how often I
   > have longed to gather your children together, as a
   > hen gathers her chicks together under her wings,
   > and you were not willing. (Luke 13:34)

Yahweh God said, "It is not good for the man to be alone. I will make a helper suitable for him." (Gen. 2:18)

3. Did Esther even know how amazing she was? No! She didn't! And that was one of her best qualities. She was unassuming and humble, not pretentious in the least. What a wonderful queen she would be!

Thus says Yahweh, "Heaven is My throne, and the earth is my footstool; what is the house that you would build for Me, and what is the place of My rest? All these things My hand has made, and so all these things came to be, declares Yahweh. But this is the one to whom I will look: he who is humble and contrite in spirit, and who trembles at my word." (Isa. 66:1–2)

Blessed are the humble, for they shall inherit the earth. (Matt. 5:5)

And from Jesus Christ who is the faithful witness, the firstborn from the dead, and the ruler of the kings of the earth. To him who loves us and has freed us from our sins by his blood. And has made us to be a Kingdom and priests to serve his God and Father—to him be glory and power forever and ever! Amen. (Rev. 1:5–6)

4. Such a gorgeous woman, with long black curls, caramel skin, and eyes like honey. The way she had gazed upon his face and body with those eyes when he had taken off his clothes made him feel so alive! And when she took off her clothes, Xerxes was barely able to stand it. Breathtaking! Esther was adorably petite in stature and totally voluptuous in form. She was simply perfect! Taking her in his arms just

felt so right! That was where she belonged! And what about her delightful little squeals and later screams of pleasure? Absolutely intoxicating to his ears!

And I am come down to deliver them out of the hand of the Egyptians, and to bring them up out of that land unto a good land and large, unto a land flowing with milk and honey; unto the place of the Canaanites, and the Hittites, and the Amorites, and the Perizzites, and the Hivites and the Jebusites. (Exod. 3:8)

You are altogether beautiful, my darling; there is no flaw in you. (Song of Solomon 4:7)

Make a joyful noise unto Yahweh, all the earth: make a loud noise, and rejoice, and sing praise. (Ps. 98:4)

The voice of joy and the voice of gladness, the voice of the bridegroom and the voice of the bride, the voice of them that shall say, 'Praise Yahweh of hosts: for Yahweh is good; for His mercy endures forever: and of them that shall bring the sacrifice of praise into the house of Yahweh. For I will cause to return the captivity of the land, as at the first, says Yahweh. (Jer. 33:11)

5. "Karshena, you know I've never much cared for your sense of humor, but whether you're joking right now or not, I will answer you. No! Absolutely not! Just in case anyone here needs a reminder, prostitution is against the law in my

kingdom. No woman should ever feel she has to sell herself. That is vile and appalling! Are we clear, everybody?"

Do not profane your daughter by making her a harlot, so that the land will not fall to harlotry and the land become full of lewdness. (Lev. 19:29)

6. "Now that I have nine new wives including Esther, I want to make a schedule to be sure I will be treating them all fairly. Esther and I will be taking political tours around the kingdom together, but we'll never be gone more than a week so I won't neglect my other wives. Since Vashti and I aren't in a relationship anymore, my remaining six wives and now the nine new ones makes fifteen. Tell Hegai the following please: I wish for him to send Esther to me every other night. That leaves fifteen days each month for my other wives. Each of those nights he can send me another wife from the other fourteen. It's important that I have time devoted to being with each of them, and so they can receive their conjugal rights as wives."

The husband should give to his wife her conjugal rights, and likewise the wife to her husband. (1 Cor. 7:3)

Chapter 10: Preparing to Be Queen

1. It was clear God had protected her and she was thankful. But did God approve of her marriage? After all, Xerxes didn't believe in her God.

Do not be yoked together with unbelievers. For what do righteousness and wickedness have in common? Or what fellowship can light have with darkness? (2 Cor. 6:14)

2. When she finally rose from the bed, she gathered up the sheet with her virgin blood. The law of Moses passed down among her people said to keep it, in case the husband later turned against her and said she hadn't been a virgin when they came together. But she saw no reason for this. Xerxes seemed to be a very good man, and he'd explained that she was his wife and family forever since coming to the palace.

    If a man takes a wife and, after sleeping with her, dislikes her and slanders her and gives her a bad name, saying, 'I married this woman, but when I approached her, I did not find proof of her virginity,' then the young woman's father and mother shall bring to the town elders at the gate proof that she was a virgin. Her father will say to the elders, 'I gave my daughter in marriage to this man, but he dislikes her. Now he has slandered her and said, 'I did not find your daughter to be a virgin.' But here is the proof of my daughter's virginity. Then her parents shall display the cloth before the elders of the town, and the elders shall take the man and punish him. They shall fine him a hundred shekels of silver and give them to the young woman's father, because this man has given an Israelite virgin a bad name. She shall continue to be his wife; he must not divorce her as long as he lives. (Deut. 22:13–19)

3. Yesterday, when she had walked this same path, she had been so nervous, she could barely think. *Thank You, God, for directing my steps when I'm nervous, and when I'm not! Thank You for always being with me!*

    In their hearts, humans plan their course, but Yahweh establishes their steps. (Prov. 16:9)

4. She gathered herself to hold her happiness in her heart. Would she be able to keep this sense of peace, or would it be taken from her again?

    Let the peace of Christ rule in your hearts, since as members of one body you were called to peace. And be thankful. (Col. 3:15)

5. Esther looked away. Those moments were private, just between her and Xerxes. "It doesn't seem right to talk about it."

    There are three things that are too amazing for me, four that I do not understand: the way of an eagle in the sky, the way of a snake on a rock, the way of a ship on the high seas, and the way of a man with a young woman. (Prov. 30:18–19)

    My dove in the clefts of the rock, in secret places of a hedge, show me your beauty, your appearance, and make me hear your voice, for your voice is sweet and your appearance is beautiful! (Song of Solomon 2:14)

6. "No spells, ever! That's not even—" Esther stopped herself midsentence. Her people didn't believe in spells. Only God has true power. All power comes from God.

    Do not turn to mediums or seek out spiritists, for you will be defiled by them. I am Yahweh your God. (Lev. 19:31)

Chapter 11: Another Father

1. "Of course, I care! To me, you girls are all my daughters. I'm a eunuch. Of course, I can't have a family like other

men. But this is my family. You all are my family. Everyone has a place in the royal family, and in the kingdom, and this is mine, and I'm thankful.'"

For there are eunuchs who were born that way, and there are eunuchs who have been made eunuchs by others—and there are eunuchs who choose to live like eunuchs for the sake of the Kingdom of heaven. The one who can accept this should accept it. (Matt. 19:12)

Better is one day in your courts than a thousand elsewhere; I would rather be a doorkeeper in the house of my God than dwell in the tents of the wicked. (Ps. 84:10)

2. "As I said, I knew you were different as soon as you got here. Way different from the others. You were the last to arrive the other day, but I knew you should go to the king first. Trust me, you have what it takes to be his queen. Anyway, the king clearly is happy with you, and I can tell from your face, you're happy with him too, right?"

But many who are first will be last, and the last first. (Mark 10:31)

3. "See? I told you! This is wonderful news, my dear! This will be so good for our family, and the kingdom too, for our king and queen to truly love each other. As much as Vashti means to us, I knew she wasn't the one for the king. It's you, Esther. You have come to bring light to the kingdom, I can tell!"

You are the light of the world. A town built on a hill cannot be hidden. Neither do people light a lamp and put it under a bowl. Instead,

they put it on its stand, and it gives light to everyone in the house. In the same way, let your light
shine before others, that they may see your good
deeds and glorify your Father in heaven. (Matt.
5:14–16)

4. "True love is more than the feeling. It's also the willingness to make sacrifices when need be, for the other person.
Vashti didn't understand that. She didn't want to leave her
banquet, even though the king had made one for her. She
wasn't able to see it from his perspective. With you, again
it's so plain to see, you are different in a good way. You
will be able to take risks for the king, when need be, in the
future, if danger comes. And he'll do the same for you."

Beloved, let us love one another, for love is
from God, and whoever loves has been born of
God and knows God. (1 John 4:7)

I appeal to you therefore, brothers, by the
mercies of God, to present your bodies as a living
sacrifice, holy and acceptable to God, which is
your spiritual worship. (Rom. 12:1)

5. "God, You have provided me another father inside this
harem. You are so generous! Thank You! Praise God, from
whom all blessings flow! Amen!"

Praise be to the God and Father of our Lord
Jesus Christ, who has blessed us in the heavenly
realms with every spiritual blessing in Christ.
(Eph. 1:3)

Also directly inspired by the hymn titled "Praise God from
Whom All Blessings Flow."

Chapter 12: Queen Esther

1. They fussed and fussed over her endlessly. Esther didn't hear a word they said. To her, she looked just the same as on the wedding night, just a different hairstyle, and new jewels for her nails. What did it matter anyway? Xerxes had already chosen her and decided she'd be queen. Would the people of Persia trust her based on her beauty alone? Esther hoped not.

    Do not let your adorning be external-the braiding of hair and the putting on of gold jewelry, or the clothing you wear-but let your adorning be the hidden person of the heart with the imperishable beauty of a gentle and quiet spirit, which in God's eyes is very precious. (1 Pet. 3:3–4)

2. Taking a deep breath, Esther placed her hand in his, and they walked together down the aisle toward the throne. Thankfully, she wasn't tripping down the aisle, and she started to feel confident walking beside her new husband in public. At the throne, Xerxes reached for a golden crown, presented it to her, and placed it on her head.

    Now the King was attracted to Esther more than to any of the other women, and she won his favor and approval more than any of the other virgins. So, he set a royal crown on her head and made her Queen instead of Vashti. (Esther 2:17)

3. *God, show me the way. You have given me power. Give me wisdom as well, I pray. As Solomon, David's son, asked for*

wisdom to rule Israel, so I also ask to be wise as queen of Persia. Amen.

Solomon answered, "You have shown great kindness to Your servant, my father David, because he was faithful to you and righteous and upright in heart. You have continued this great kindness to him and have given him a son to sit on his throne this very day. Now, Yahweh my God, You have made Your servant king in place of my father David. But I am only a little child and do not know how to carry out my duties. Your servant is here among the people You have chosen, a great people, too numerous to count or number. So, give Your servant a discerning heart to govern Your people and to distinguish between right and wrong. For who is able to govern this great people of Yours?" (1 Kings 3:6–9)

Chapter 13: King and Queen Together

1. After the ceremony, there had been a banquet in the public banquet hall. She had sat next to Xerxes, and her head had been spinning with excitement and happiness.

    And the King gave a great banquet, Esther's banquet, for all his nobles and officials. (Esther 2:18)

2. *God, I know I can't be naked when I walk to the bridal chamber of course! Adam and Eve were naked in the Garden together. But I can do the next best thing for Xerxes, reassuring him of how I feel, that I am truly grateful for him and really with him. And being naked under my dress is the symbol of that, plus Xerxes will like it and it will be fun! Please be with*

me and let me speak well to my husband tonight. In Your name, I pray!

And the man and his wife were both naked,
and they felt no shame. (Gen. 2:25)

Chapter 14: Royal Life, Royal Marriage

1. Esther traveled with Xerxes quite a bit to various parts of the empire, both far and near from the palace. What a privilege and honor to accompany her husband, the king, to serve their people, together! Xerxes asked her what they could do to help people, especially women and children, be safer and healthier throughout Persia. It had really stuck with him how she said she hadn't felt safe in her life before she'd married him. To address this, they put together various programs to support the poor, children, orphans, widows, and women in general.

   Religion that God our Father accepts as
   pure and faultless is this: to look after orphans
   and widows in their distress and to keep oneself
   from being polluted by the world. (James 1:27)

2. Esther arranged for visits in the outer courtyard of the court of women for the other wives with their families too, plus for her maids and all the women who worked there to see their families. She loved using her queen privileges to bring happiness, not just for her, but for the other ladies living and working in the harem as well.

   After she became Queen, Xerxes had a new room made for her on the upper level of the harem, with a balcony overlooking the courtyard. Delighted with this gift, she had given her old room downstairs to her seven maids. She didn't need that room anymore, and it would be nice for them to have their own space. Xerxes also gave Esther

her own personal eunuch servant named Hathak. He came to be like a brother to Esther, like her maids had become like younger sisters. How nice to have siblings for the first time in her life! Indeed, she felt favored and blessed to have come to this royal family!

Do nothing out of selfish ambition or vain conceit. Rather, in humility value others above yourselves, not looking to your own interests but each of you to the interests of others. (Phil. 2:3–4)

Hathak, one of the King's eunuchs assigned to attend her. (Esther 4:5)

3. "Of course. Just one more thing. Xerxes never told me he loved me because he didn't, even though he wanted to and he tried so hard. But everyone knows he loves you and I'm sure he will tell you soon if he hasn't already."

In the last days, God says, I will pour out My spirit on all people. Your sons and daughters will prophesy, your young men will see visions, your old men will dream dreams. (Acts 2:17)

Chapter 15: A Plot Discovered

1. Mordecai had never been more joyful! He was newlywed to Leenah, and both he and Esther were now happily married. From what he saw and heard of Xerxes, he seemed to be a good man. It seemed clear the man loved her, and she him. God had provided such a good life for them both! Who

would have thought they'd both find love in a foreign land without their parents? God truly works wonders!

> You are the God Who works wonders. (Ps. 77:13–14)

2. "His life with Leenah was much more comfortable than the life he'd lived while raising Esther. Thanks to Esther and Xerxes' generous help and gifts, both Leenah's bakery business and his butcher shop were doing so much better. He and Leenah were even able to renovate the house after she moved in. Best of all, in doing so, he was finally able to say goodbye to those hideous, bloodstained front steps. Thanks be to God! He'd never forget that day, or the beloved memory of his and Esther's parents. Still, what a joy to not have that constant, sad reminder literally on his doorstep!

> He proclaimed a holiday throughout the provinces and distributed gifts with royal liberality. (Esther 2:18)

3. That also meant he no longer had to lie about the bloodstains since they were now gone. *Lord, forgive me for breaking your commandment to always tell the truth! You know I did so in order to keep Esther and I safe, and now I thank You for Your forgiveness and compassion, as well as no longer having to lie to protect us! Amen!*

> You shall not bear false witness against your neighbor. (Exod. 20:16)

> The Lord our God is merciful and forgiving, even though we have rebelled against Him. (Dan. 9:9)

4. "Here's the plan! The king will most likely be in the bridal chamber with the queen. We'll pose as servants, bringing them refreshments, and when they open the door, we attack! First, we kill the king and then we enjoy his wife! Queen Esther of Persia, indeed!"

   During the time Mordecai was sitting at the King's gate, Bigthana and Teresh, two of the King's officers who guarded the doorway, became angry and conspired to assassinate King Xerxes. (Esther 2:21)

5. They laughed and laughed. Mordecai was incredulous. How could these men be so deplorable, and planning such a despicable plot! A moment ago, he'd been basking in the joy of his and Esther's new life, and now it had all come crashing down! God, are we returning to the days of Noah!

   Just as it was in the days of Noah, so also will it be in the days of the son of man. (Luke 17:26)

6. "Lord, let me fly as if on eagles' wings! Please!"

   But those who hope in Yahweh will renew their strength. They will soar on wings like eagles; they will run and not grow weary, they will walk and not be faint. (Isa. 40:31)

7. Mordecai took off running. He had run to save Esther when she was a baby, and he would do the same now! He couldn't get to the court of women gate fast enough!
   God, You are my only hope! Send Esther out, now!

   For You have been my hope, sovereign Yahweh, my confidence since my youth. (Ps. 71:5)

Chapter 16: Warning the Queen

1. "Like always, I was walking past the king's gate on my way here. I heard two men, the guards at the door, talking. Their names are Bigthana and Teresh."

   During the time Mordecai was sitting at the King's gate, Bigthana and Teresh, two of the King's officers who guarded the doorway, became angry and conspired to assassinate King Xerxes. But Mordecai found out about the plot and told Queen Esther, who in turn reported it to the King, giving credit to Mordecai. (Esther 2:21–22)

Chapter 17: God Save the King

Title inspired by "God Save the Queen," British national anthem.

1. "My king, may you live forever!"

   Daniel answered, "May the King live forever!" (Dan. 6:21)

2. "I've heard enough! Guards, take them outside and hang them up on a tree! You will not hurt me, or the queen, let justice be done to put evil away from the kingdom!"

   And when the report was investigated and found to be true, the two officials were impaled on poles. (Esther 2:23)

   And if a man has committed a crime punishable by death and he is put to death, and you hang him on a tree, his body shall not remain all night on the tree, but you shall bury him the next day, for a hanged man is cursed by God. You shall not defile the land that Yahweh your God is giving you for an inheritance. (Deut. 21:22–23)

The hands of the witnesses must be the first in putting that person to death, and then the hands of all the people. You must purge the evil from among you. (Deut. 17:7)

Chapter 18: Mordecai Reveals His Faith

1. "Haman, thank you for your help yesterday. You really stepped up in my moment of need to protect both me and the queen. You clearly took the lead in the execution of the traitors and getting rid of them as soon as possible. I'd like to promote you to my second-in-command. How's that?"

    After these events, King Xerxes honored Haman son of Hammedatha, the Agagite, elevating him and giving him a seat of honor higher than that of all the other nobles. (Esther 3:1)

2. "All should bow down and do reverence to Haman, my new second-in-command! Yesterday, he came through to bring the traitors to justice, and protect myself and the Queen! Respect and bow to him when you see him in my gate!"

    All the royal officials at the King's gate knelt down and paid honor to Haman, for the King had commanded this concerning him. (Esther 3:2)

3. "Sir, I respect you are the king's choice for second-in-command, and I congratulate you on that. But I cannot bow down to anyone but God. Because I am a Jew."

    But Mordecai would not kneel down or pay him honor. (Esther 3:2)

Then the royal officials at the King's gate asked Mordecai, "Why do you disobey the King's command?" Day after day they spoke to him but he refused to comply. Therefore, they told Haman about it to see whether Mordecai's behavior would be tolerated, for he had told them he was a Jew. (Esther 3:3–4)

Chapter 19: A Plot against the Jews

1. "You have a big head, you just need to learn how to use it, my husband. You're close to the king now, second-in-command. Tell him there is a group of people who have it out against the laws of Persia who won't obey. Mordecai wouldn't obey the order to do reverence to you, and he's a Jew, so it's just a tiny stretch of the truth, is it not?"

   When Haman saw that Mordecai would not kneel down or pay him honor, he was enraged. Yet having learned who Mordecai's people were, he scorned the idea of killing only Mordecai. Instead, Haman looked for a way to destroy all Mordecai's people, the Jews, throughout the whole Kingdom of Xerxes. (Esther 3:5–6)

2. "Do I have to do everything around here! Look, it's the only way to get what we want, so yes, this is what must be done! And you know what? Shame on that Mordecai for not reverencing my husband. We should prepare something really special for him, a special way out, a torturous death. Not just torturous but humiliating too! He should be hung in the public square just like those two traitors!

Tomorrow, see to it that you have a hanging post set up, fifty feet high. That's where he can meet his end!"

His wife Zeresh and all his friends said to him, "Have a pole set up, reaching to a height of fifty cubits, and ask the King in the morning to have Mordecai impaled on it." (Esther 5:14)

Chapter 20: Leenah and Mordecai at Home

1. "Well, not to worry. I'm sure it'll all be fine. Esther is queen and you said so yourself that the king loves her. No harm should come her way. And as for you, you're clearly feeling a lot better and safer. Now that I've seen you're in a much better place, I can tell you some happy news! I've actually been getting a lot of customers at the shop lately who are talking openly about being Jewish. They're not scared anymore! We have so many brothers and sisters in faith all around us and didn't even know it! Praise Yahweh!"

"Who are my mother and my brothers?" he asked. Then he looked at those seated in a circle around him and said, "Here are my mother and my brothers! Whoever does God's will is my brother and sister and mother!" (Mark 3:33–35)

How wonderful and pleasant it is when brothers live together in harmony! (Ps. 133:1)

Chapter 21: Tricking the King

1. "Your Majesty, some disturbing news has come to my attention. There is a people scattered throughout the kingdom who keep themselves separate. They have different customs, and they don't respect your laws! It's clearly not in your best

interest to put up with this people. Therefore, if I may so humbly suggest, you should make a decree to destroy them."

Then Haman said to King Xerxes, "There is a certain people dispersed among the peoples in all the provinces of your Kingdom who keep themselves separate. Their customs are different from those of all other people, and they do not obey the King's laws; it is not in the King's best interest to tolerate them. If it pleases the King, let a decree be issued to destroy them, and I will give ten thousand talents of silver to the King's administrators for the royal treasury." (Esther 3:8–9)

2. "All right, Haman, if this is really true, then yes, something should be done about it, before it gets out of hand. It seems these people haven't been identified by name yet. Let's not let it get to that point then, right? Listen, take my ring and make the order, signing it with my hand thereby. As soon as you're done, come back here. We have many other important things to discuss today in the throne room with other nobles and politicians. Don't waste too much time on something that should be easy to take care of."

So, the King took his signet ring from his finger and gave it to Haman son of Hammedatha, the Agagite, the enemy of the Jews. "Keep the money," the King said to Haman, "and do with the people as you please." (Esther 3:10–11)

Chapter 22: What's the Matter with Mordecai?

1. Even as she prayed, Esther knew something else was bothering her. It had been almost a month since she'd seen her Xerxes. She missed him so much her heart ached.

> But thirty days have passed since I was
> called to go to the King. (Esther 4:11)

2. "But I will be patient. Love is patient. He told me he wouldn't let a month pass without sending for me, so only a few days left."

> Love is patient, love is kind. It does not
> envy, it does not boast, it is not proud. (1 Cor.
> 13:4)

3. Esther looked away into the distance, her thoughts turning to Mordecai. Suddenly, as if in direct answer to her thoughts, he appeared! To her surprise, he was wearing sackcloth and ashes, the apparel of one who is in mourning!

> When Esther's eunuchs and female attendants came and told her about Mordecai, she
> was in great distress. She sent clothes for him to
> put on instead of his sackcloth, but he would not
> accept them. (Esther 4:4)

4. "Thanks so much for delivering me the message, Hathak! We all know it is against the law for anyone to enter the throne room, unless the king has called for them. As I said, Xerxes hasn't called for me for almost a month at this point, but I can't wait any longer! I must tell him of this, and I know how I will do it. First, I will tell him who I am and then reveal this plot. God made me queen for a reason, and I have to fight for my people. If not, how can I even call myself a queen! I will do what is right! I know Xerxes loves me and won't want to kill me for entering the throne room without permission beforehand, but if someone else says otherwise and if I have to die, so be it. Here's what I'll do, tell this to Mordecai. Tell him to gather up all the Jews in the region and fast, not drinking or eating for three days.

Hathak, you and I and my maids will do the same. At the end of the three days, I will go to the king. If I die, at least I will die doing something for my people."

Then Esther sent this reply to Mordecai: "Go, gather together all the Jews that are in Susa, and fast for me. Do not eat or drink for three days, night or day. I and my attendants will fast as you do. When this is done, I will go to the King, even though it is against the law. And if I perish, I perish." (Esther 4:15–16)

Chapter 23: Queen before the King

1. Bright and early on the third day, Esther rose, bathed, and dressed, and put on her royal garments. Today was the first anniversary of her wedding night with Xerxes. Now, it was time to go to him again, but she would tell him who she really was. She had no fear, only faith. Perfect love casts out fear after all, and that's what she felt for this man.

On the third day, Esther put on her royal robes and stood in the inner court of the Palace, in front of the King's hall. The King was sitting on his royal throne, in front of the entrance. When he saw Queen Esther standing in the court, he was pleased with her, and held out to her the gold scepter that was in his hand. So, Esther approached and touched the tip of the scepter. (Esther 5:1–2)

There is no fear in love. But perfect love drives out fear, because fear has to do with punishment. The one who fears is not made perfect in love. (1 John 4:18)

2. Esther ran to him then, as if she were a little girl!

    Casting all your care upon Him, for he cares
    for you. (1 Pet. 5:7)

Chapter 24: Esther Gives Her Whole Heart

1. "Don't apologize; it's okay! You are very young and it can
    take a little while."

    So, neither the one who plants nor the
    one who waters is anything, but only God, who
    makes things grow. (1 Cor. 3:7)

2. "My uncle Mordecai always wanted me to be safe, and
    since our parents were killed for being Jews when I was
    only three, he raised me to never tell anyone, even a hus-
    band, about my origins. I'm so sorry, Xerxes."

    Esther had not revealed her nationality and
    family background, because Mordecai had for-
    bidden her to do so. (Esther 2:10)

3. "I am so sorry too for what you've been through, Esther!
    And it goes even deeper than that, right? I know Hebrews
    have had a difficult history. Pharaoh was cowardly enough
    to have your babies put to death, out of fear of rebellion. I
    guess your people have lived in fear of extermination for so
    long, it's just always there on some level. I think I under-
    stand that, and no, this isn't something I hold against you."

    Then Pharoah gave this order to all his peo-
    ple: "Every Hebrew boy that is born you must
    throw into the Nile, but let every girl live." (Exod.
    1:22)

4. "And let me be very clear about this. When I say God, I am speaking about your God. The God of Abraham, Isaac, and Jacob."

   "I am the God of your ancestors. The God of Abraham, Isaac, and Jacob." Moses hid his face because he was afraid to look at God. (Exod. 3:6)

5. As they made love, Esther fully surrendered her heart to Xerxes.

   For where your treasure is, there your heart will be also. (Matt. 6:21)

Chapter 25: Mordecai Is Honored by the King

1. As he pondered all this, he came across a paper that summarized the events of when Mordecai had discovered Bigthana and Teresh's plot on his life and to hurt the queen. Had nothing been done to honor and reward Mordecai? How could he have overlooked this? He'd honored Haman for dragging the traitors to the trees to be killed, but he'd forgotten to recognize Mordecai! Better late than never. *I will raise up Mordecai tomorrow, first thing.* With that, he went back to sleep beside his beloved Esther.

   That night the King could not sleep; so, he ordered the book of the chronicles, the record of his reign, to be brought in and read to him. It was found recorded there that Mordecai had exposed Bigthana and Teresh, two of the King's officers who guarded the doorway, who had conspired to assassinate King Xerxes. (Esther 6:1–2)

2. "Haman, what should be done for the man who the king delights to honor?"

Haman's eyes brightened, and it was clear he thought the king was speaking of him. *Not so*, thought Xerxes, *not this time.*

"I would say, bring a royal robe of the king's for him, along with the king's horse, plus, give him a royal crest. Then, have one of the king's nobles ride with him throughout the streets, proclaiming, 'This is a man the king delights to honor!'"

"Excellent. Haman, please go get Mordecai the Jew outside the king's gate, and do everything you have said. Spare no detail you have mentioned. Go!"

Frowning, Haman slowly turned around and reluctantly did all that was asked of him. Mordecai the Jew was to be honored while he was humiliated to do this for the man who wouldn't bow down to him. He couldn't believe how cruel and unjust this was!

When Haman entered, the King asked him, "What should be done for the man the King delights to honor?" Now Haman thought to himself, "Who is there that the King would rather honor than me?" So, he answered the King, "For the man the King delights to honor, have them bring a royal robe the King has worn and a horse the King has ridden, one with a royal crest placed upon his head. Then let the robe and horse be entrusted to one of the King's most noble princes. Let them robe the man the King delights to honor, and lead him on the horse through the city streets, proclaiming before him, "This is what is done for the man the King delights to honor!" (Esther 6:6–9)

3. Meanwhile, Esther was watching everything from the window of the bridal chamber. She saw Mordecai being

escorted through the city in a royal robe and crest. How nice that Xerxes had honored her uncle! What a kind and fitting gesture. She was grinning from ear to ear for pride. *Thank You, God. Indeed, You have lifted up the lowly, first me, and now my uncle. God be praised!*

Yahweh lifts up the humble, he casts the wicked to the ground. (Ps. 147:6)

Chapter 26: The Banquet

1. "What do you want most, Esther? You know I would give you anything, even half the kingdom as I told you before."

   "Xerxes, you know I don't need anything. I have everything I need, and more. But since you asked, there is something more I must tell you."

   She raised her voice so the entire room would hear. This was the time to speak loudly to expose the evil plot in the sight and ears of everyone there.

   "If it pleases the king, let my life and the life of my people be given to me. Let us be saved! For we have been sold, my people and I, to be killed!"

   So, the King and Haman went to Queen Esther's banquet, and as they were drinking wine on the second day, the King again asked, "Queen Esther, what is your petition? It will be given you. What is your request? Even up to half the Kingdom, it will be granted." Then Queen Esther answered, "If I have found favor with you, your Majesty, and if it pleases you, grant me my life—this is my peti- tion. And spare my people—this is my request. For I and my people have been sold to be destroyed, killed and annihilated." (Esther 7:1–4)

2. "Who is this man, and where is he! Who would dare to do such a thing!"

    Esther pointed her finger at Haman. "It is this wicked Haman who is both our adversary and enemy!"

    King Xerxes asked Queen Esther, "Who is he? Where is he—the man who has dared to do such a thing?" Esther said, "An adversary and enemy! This vile Haman!" (Esther 7:5–6)

3. Xerxes was so upset he got up from the table and left, walking outside to the palace garden, pacing angrily back and forth. When he couldn't take it anymore, he fell to his knees. He began to pray out loud with tears streaming down his face.

    The King got up in a rage, left his wine and went out into the Palace Garden. (Esther 7:7)

4. *The man I thought was my friend, who is eating at the table next to my Esther, wants to kill her and her people, Your people! God, I can't handle this. I can't fix all my mistakes. I'm not strong enough on my own! Please, God, I need You! I know You have spoken to Your people in the past, and I don't know if You will speak to me now, but please give me a sign so I can know what to do! I am weak, but You are strong! Help me, God!*

    Even my close friend, someone I trusted, who shared my bread, has turned against me. (Ps. 41:9)

    For when I am weak, then I am strong. (2 Cor. 12:10)

5. At that moment, Xerxes returned, aghast at what he saw. Was this man touching his beloved Esther! He ran at him, grabbed him by the throat, and pulled Haman off of Esther.

"Don't you ever come near my queen! How dare you!" He flung Haman to the ground.

At that moment, a servant approached Xerxes, gently placing a hand on his shoulder.

"Yes, Harbona, what is it?"

"Your Majesty, if I may, look outside at that hanging post fifty feet high this Haman has constructed. What do you think we should do with him?"

Without hesitation, Xerxes yelled, "Hang him on it! Get him out of here, now!"

The guards took Haman away, kicking and screaming.

For whoever touches you touches the apple of His eye. (Zech. 2:8)

Just as the King returned from the Palace Garden to the banquet hall, Haman was falling on the couch where Esther was reclining. The King exclaimed, "Will he even molest the Queen while she is with me in the house?" As soon as the word left the King's mouth, they covered Haman's face. Then Harbona, one of the eunuchs attending the King, said, "A pole reaching to the height of fifty cubits stands by Haman's house. He had it set up for Mordecai, who spoke up to help the King." The King said, "Impale him on it!" (Esther 7:8–9)

6. "He was indeed evil, a trickster and a liar! It's not about you. He was a bad man. He was jealous and covetous. Sometimes, bad people are jealous of good people. He was also envious of my uncle, which is how this all started."

He has always hated the truth, because there is no truth in him. When he lies, it is consistent with his character; for he is a liar and the father of lies. (John 8:44)

For he knew that for envy they had delivered him. (Matt. 27:18)

7. "I hardly feel like a hero right now, Esther! You're being so kind and generous as always. I said I would always protect you, and thankfully I wasn't too late. Thanks be to God! I'll issue an order to reverse the plot Haman concocted. Your parents were right to name you after a myrtle tree. You have enriched and grown my heart, our family, and our kingdom, as a myrtle tree reaches up to God in heaven. You are a hero too, my love. Now come with me."

Now write another decree in the King's name in behalf of the Jews As it seems best to you, and seal it with the King's signet ring. (Esther 8:8)

8. Xerxes took Esther's hand in his. They walked together to the balcony and looked over their kingdom God had given them. The enemy was now dead. They would be able to rest, live, work, love, and worship God, now, in peace. Amen and amen!

The last enemy to be destroyed is death. (1 Cor. 15:26)

For the grace of God has appeared, bringing salvation for all people. (Titus 2:11)

Praise be to Yahweh forever! Amen and amen. (Ps. 89:52)

ABOUT THE AUTHOR

Patricia Herdoiza Hernández is a professor of psychology. Fascinated by the Bible stories since she was a child, she has always loved to imagine these accounts through the eyes of the people who lived them. She was raised Catholic and taught the Bible stories by her beloved deceased *nonna* (grandmother) and decided to be baptized a Christadelphian at the age of twenty-seven. A few years later, she discovered her passion for writing fan fiction accounts of these tales, her main goal being to point the audience toward Christ. She loves to preach the Gospel through relating the Bible stories as seen through her eyes. Her profession as a psychology professor gives her insight, aiding the perspective and bringing these stories to life on the human level. Patricia was born and raised in Maryland, where she lives with her husband, Elías, and their daughter, Camila. The photo is from Patricia's July 2022 trip to Israel, the promised land, with her husband and daughter.